American Challenges in the Obama Era Part 2

Commentary, Spoken Word and Essays

By Larry Ukali Johnson-Redd

The Reading Glass Books
(888) 420-3050
www.readingglassbooks.com
fulfillment@readingglassbooks.com

American Challenges in the Obama Era Part ll
Commentary, Essays and Spokenword

By Larry Ukali Johnson-Redd

This book is dedicated to my mom and siblings but also all victims of police and vigilante violence and terror. This book is also dedicated to the new majority groups and all progressives in America and all progressives all over the world who fight for economic justice, political justice and human rights so we can enjoy a state of liberation all over the world while progressives and new majority groups continue to work for the end of colonialism that precedes world liberation.

Table of Contents

As we get going in late January 2014, we must remember that something horrible happened in the last days of the Bush (the son)'s administration that has had a lasting effect on the American Economy and the steps taken by the Obama Administration and the declining Republican opposition. I say declining only because the population in base of the Republicans, old, white and rich is on the decline. Obviously the new majority is on the rise but the Republicans in this their off-season still have control of the House of Representatives and exercise a strong hand in negotiations with the Democrats in the Senate and the Obama Administration.

No doubt the Democratic party in order to remain relevant to the new majority consisting of Immigrants, progressive women, growing minorities of color Latinos, Asians, Native Americans and African-Americans as well as progressive white youth and the middle class.

The new majority has put Obama in office both times and deserves some rewards of the battles at the polls especially African-Americans who still remain Americas last hired and first fired.

This new Obama Administration though born with the physical lift and debt ceiling negotiations at the beginning of this term must go beyond the issues and reward new majority voters and the communities with jobs, economic development and efforts to renew Americas infrastructure while assisting effects of the multinationals and the massive forces of globalization as well as global capitalism to bring the ATT Call Center as well as the other jobs the Bush Administration encouraged multinationals to outsource American jobs and economic assets overseas. To be sure President Obama has advocated for the renewal of America s ailing infrastructure but the Republicans and conservative Democrats blocked every effort while the ailing bridges continue crumbling as a monument to divided government.

This is the massive agenda and challenge faced by the second term of the Obama Administration.

If the Obama Administration is a child of the new majority and it is then surely the agenda of the new majority including immigration reform and inner city economic revitalization must be seen by the new majority as a new majority issues being fought for tooth and nail by the Obama Administration and any progressive republican (?) this new majority may abandon the traditional democratic party.

Why do I Say New Majority?

The new demographic emerging in America forecast the growing power of the new majority projecting that America becomes a majority non-white society by 2045 or after 2048.

When that projection emerged in 2000, I nearly wrote a book projecting a new and first Black present in 2042 however the Obama candidacy and election made me happy I did not complete that proposed novel in 2000. In both elections the Obama Administration won without the majority of the votes of white Americans but with votes of the new majority. Now the Obama Administration has to work for the New Majority and not for the corporations however Monsanto's and other corporations are having a field day. And it could be said Black issues and Black lives are under attack through discrimination in employment, police assassinations, Trayvon Martin type vigilante killings, voter suppression laws enacted by republicans to name a few.

Realization of new majority values objectives and legislation compromising where necessary with Republican controlled legislature-progressives and new majority must vote and organize to help an overall effort to vote the exiting Congress out and add in a new Congress, (I hope that house majority will not be controlled by the Republicans for too much longer) . Immigration reform and end to the massive deportation of the first Obama Administration and a path to citizenship for 12 million illegal must be the primary objective for the new majority and Obama Administration. However it appears that this new majority must learn better and more effective ways of negotiating with whoever is in power and more than that should consider the formation of the new majority party.

Economic development for the inner city unemployed and rural poor must be the next objective. There is no time for 1of those priorities at a time both must be seen as priorities by new majority voters or they will begin to look at the Obama Administration and democratic party are the same as the republican party. This is a major challenge for Present Obama, his administration, the democratic party and America as a whole.

Now the Obama has many people who doubt his authentic American birth from the American right and a few from the center. These crazy right wing racists are called the" Birthers" Movement. Donald Trump is the leader. Obama receives criticism from the skeptics of the new majority, the republicans and many African American leaders. When it comes to the election where Obama received 96% of the African-American vote, Many African-Americans who live in the shadows didn't vote because of felonies or inability to present newly republican inspired identification requirement/voter suppression laws are counting on the democratic party becoming more like the envisioned new majority party so they can come out of the shadows. Many so called illegal aliens would like to come out of the shadows and this is the table that is set at the beginning of the second term of the Obama administration.

The Germans are still vilified for killing 6 million Jews, B blacks and browns. American has got to escape from the present policies of deporting 1200000 human beings or it will share it will share the stench with Nazi Germany because that county operates out of a prejudice perspective when it comes to the 6 million Jews. There is still a need to compensate The African- American victims of slavery through the western hemisphere

Despite America electing a black man twice, America can hope to be a post racial society tomorrow because America as a whole today continues to treat most African Americans with derision; i.e. racial discrimination, police brutality, two tier health care and a two tier educational system. As well as a first fired last hired policies those are official and unofficial period. And the latest instances of police brutality, terror and brutality continue to be shown on you-tube and network T.V.- many times white racism continues to haunt notions of a post racist society.

The Successful Re-election of the First African-American :President Barack Hussein Obama.

I must begin by saying that as a working person, I worked full time for only 1 ½ year of the first four year term despite all of my education, experience and a comprehensive job search.

During the other 2 ½ years of the first term, I worked two part-time jobs and fought with the unemployment laws and beau racy that prefers you either not work and collect the meager unemployment. If you work part-time like many do these days you will find a ready conflict with the unemployment people/ department who want to work only part-time anyway-especially when your bills require full time job income.

So the reelection of the President Obama over his rival, Romny and the republicans took place in 2012. The atmosphere was polluted because many republican governors and republican state legislators were trying to scare black and browns from voting with the new requirements to have a government issued I.D. to vote.

It must be said this was un-presented ugly, this move was meant to disqualify enough voters to deliver a victory to Romny and the republicans over Obama. The next thing you know in early March people petitioned the Supreme Court to knock out the voting rights act. However it did not happen that way as 96% of African American voters, voted for Obama and 69% of Hispanic voters also voted for Obama.

I voted for Mr. Obama fearing mainly it would be my last time for a while or maybe forever to vote for a brother despite only working part-time, despite seeking full time work for my full time bills.

The Challenge of the Future

Where is the love
That helped us survive
Challenges of a new generation
Headed for self annihilation

Why aren't we united?
Fighting for voting rights
IN most of us remember those
Who hung like kites

Now we are killing each other
Like we are not sister and brother
And it spread to the human family
Bring pain and death to the human family

Our ancestors were killed by KKK
look at what were doing this very day
Is the new black and brown KKK or CIA?
Why do you continue to act this way

A poor brother killed by another
We will not make
Progress or cant we try something different
And make people content

We must break a negative pattern
People's liberation
Is better than self annihilation
For all and every nation
Put aside self annihilation

Challenge young new generation

Fight for our rights
Liberation new and powerful generation
Take care of our families
Is more important for the oppressed to be free

In the new society let peace and development reign
Let today's poor people be kings and queens tomorrow
Because life is worth more than the way we live
When violence and death is all we give

Respect your elders and senior citizens
You will find they really are youth's best friends
It's all about our rights
Raise your sights

Make progress in human developments
Not self annihilation
not killing our own kind
But people's liberation

Second Term of the Obama Administration

If the Obama Administrations a child of the new majority and it is them surely the agenda of the new majority including immigration reform and inner city economic revitalization must be seen by the new majority as a new reality of issues being fought for tooth and nail by the Obama Administration and progressive republicans or this new majority may abandon the traditional democratic party.

Why do I Say New Majority?

The new demographic emerging in America forecast the growing power of the new majority projecting that America becomes a majority non-white society after 2048. When that projection emerged in 2000, I nearly wrote a book projecting a new and first Black president in 2042 however the Obama candidacy and election made me happy I did not complete that proposed novel in 20000. In both elections the Obama Administration won without the majority of the votes of White Americans but with votes of the new majority. Now the Obama Administration has to work for the realization of New Majority values, objectives and legislation compromising where necessary within the different groups of the new majority.

Even though Republican controlled house this must change. Immigration reform and an end to the massive deportation of the first Obama Administration and a path to citizenship for 12 million illegal must be a primary objective for the new majority and Obama Administration.

Economic development for the inner city unemployed and rural poor must be the next objective. There is no time for 1 of these priorities at a time both must be seen as priorities by the new majority voters or they will begin to look at the Obama Administration and democratic party as the same as the Republican party. This is a major challenge for President Obama his administration, the Democratic Party and America as a whole.

Now Obama has many people who doubt his authentic US born citizenship from the American right led by Donald Trump. Many call themselves Birthers. Obama receives criticism from the skeptics of the new majority, the republicans and many African American leaders. When it came to the election Obama received 96% of the African American vote. Many African- Americans who live in the shadows did not vote because of felonies or inability to present newly republican inspired identification requirement are counting on the Democratic party becoming more like envisioned new majority party so they can come out of the shadows. Many illegal aliens would like to come out of the shadows and this is the table that is set at the beginning of the second term of the Obama Administration.

The Germans are still vilified for killing 6 million Jews and blacks and browns. America has got to escape from the present policy of deporting 12 million human beings or it will share the stench with Nazi, Germany because both countries operate out of a racist perspective when it comes to the 6 or 12 million. Despite America electing a Blackman 2 times America can hope to be a post racial society tomorrow because America as a whole continues to teach most African-Americans with racism today i.e. racial discrimination, police brutality, 2 lack of healthcare., 2 tier educational system, first fired, last hired polices official and unofficial and the list of racism ghost continues to haunt notions of a past racial society.

While the Senate is debating Immigration reform the plan that appears to be emerging includes too many processes and an evasive path to citizenship. When it should be obvious that a complete amnesty: is appropriate and necessary for our new majority brothers and sisters, while some form of closing the border could be considered. But only based on the 12 million people already here receive amnesty and a path to citizenship.

First the proposal being discussed here in April 2013 includes factors like requiring the militarization of the boarder as the first priority. The long boarder would be easier to militarize without cuts required be Senate and the over 650 US military base all around the world.

The proposed bill also includes a 13 year path to citizenship. There is talk of requiring people to learn English. I did not like the late Present Ronald Reagan. Obama has stated some aspect of liking Reagan.

I felt Regan liked both Bush I and Bush II did not care about the interest of the Black or Brown people. But Reagan gave immigrants a full pardon mostly so he could recruit right wing anti-Castro Cubans into the Republican party and the Congress did not block Reagan. We ll I am calling on Present Obama to declare an amnesty for all illegal immigrants in the U.S.A. and that preparation be made by the Census, ICE, Homeland Security and other relevant agonies of the Federal, state and local governments to register them all in 90 days as an act of human kindness. While the boarders to the north and south are militarized with troops returning from Iraq and Afghanistan. As I urge Obama to make a grand attempt. I know the republicans will oppose the proposed initially however somewhere during the process they will get on board or become the smaller minority power with no change to win the presidency.

I strongly urge African American to support Present Obama on this along with the rest of the new majority noting that the old majority lead by the republicans will oppose this proposal.

The Rage of Murder by American Police 2013 to 2015 in Obama's second term of the open violation of African American Human Rights in Obama's second term.

These American police have been killing or assassinating African Americans since beginning of policing in American society. They have been getting away with it facing no accountability just like the slave catcher predecessors who have been killing African Americans without accountability. This brutal treatment of African Americans in particular but to certain extant other brown people is a complete disgrace on the American flag, the American Constitutional system and of laws and American as a country.

This continuing murder of African Americans like Larry Lumpkins in San Francisco in 1986 to Mike Brown in 2014 is a national problem for American whenever American points it's finger to any other country like China because they call American out for Americas hypocrisy violating African American Human Rights for the last 500 years in Africa, the Caribbean, Central and South American as well as the belly of the beast the United States of America.

I am a former government teacher in Nigeria. After my training in Academics particularly government my undergraduate major, America violated constitutional principles everyday on the streets of America.

The itchy trigger fingers violates the Human Rights of African Americans in every region of American so what we have is an American National problem. African Americans as a nation is inside the American nation. African America is a cultural, political and human nation within the USA nation. This and our history make us one of the most unique nations /populations in history.

As a nation, what will we do about this national problem of police brutality especially when you add the murder by white vigilantes like the killing of Trayvon Martin in Georgia?

How can American claim to be the leader of the so called free world with the worst Human Rights record in the world, from slavery to modern day police brutality? In America we all remember the late Sean Bell of New York or we should.

What has Obama done about it nothing! He has used his bully pulpit? Very little. Even in Charleston instead of him calling a racist motivated murder, Obama sought to minimize it by calling it simply another mass murder. No cops are arrested during his tenure for Human Rights violations. One police is arrested in South Carolina when a beautiful Caribbean brother who videotaped the murder and cover up where this policeman tried to put his Taser on the dead victim after killing him in cold blood.

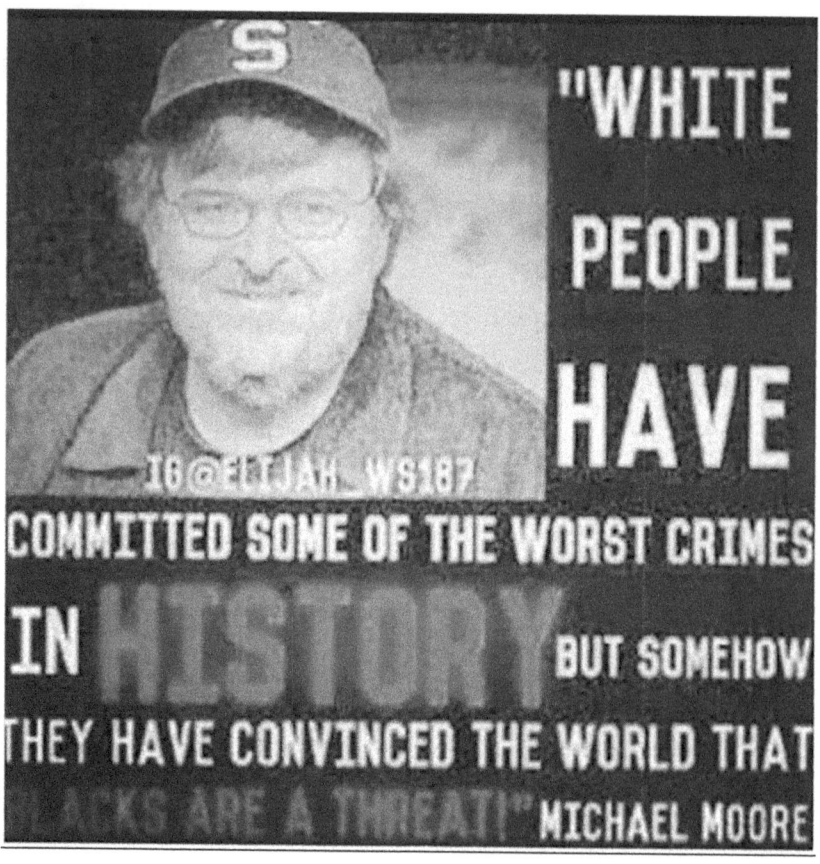

"WHITE PEOPLE HAVE COMMITTED SOME OF THE WORST CRIMES IN HISTORY BUT SOMEHOW THEY HAVE CONVINCED THE WORLD THAT BLACKS ARE A THREAT!" MICHAEL MOORE

What can we do about it as African Americans who witness a powerless Obama, tried to stop, block, defuse or punish murders of mostly African American men, women, and sometimes children all over this country. So again I ask what can African American's do all over America.

In the year 2015 alone, it is well documented that across the country more than 700 people have been injured or killed by police. In Baltimore MD. It was Freddie Gray. In Texas it was Sandra Bland who was beaten into the ground by male deputies. We all have seen the videos. In New York it was Eric Gardener on Staten Island in New York, and the mass incarceration of Black is intolerable in 2015.

The person terrorized and killed is usually a person of color. Although several Latino/Mexicans have been killed however most often the victims of police terror/brutality are African Americans. I know I can't list them all; however I do remember Michael Black a preteen killed in Oakland, CA while playing with a toy gun in the eighties. There is a long history of police terror. Michal Black's murder in the 1980's mirrors the recent murder of TAMIR RICE in Cleveland and Alex Lopez in Napa County because all of these victims of Police Terror that carried toy guns when killed by police.

There was a sister names Ruth Love who was killed by police in 1979 while gardening. Again the history of murder by police of African Americans goes back to slavery where policing of slaves occurred by slave catchers, slave trackers, and slave makers. The police like SFPD have done a lot more to keep the horror and stress of slavery with their racist texts. Police documented law breaking conspiracies range from post Katrina killings in New Orleans, ramparts in Los Angeles as well as the well-known beating of Rodney King. I remember as a teen, the murder of Mathew Johnson by SFPD that began the Hunter's Point riot of 1966 in San Francisco, CA. In Oakland too there has been too many violent murders and even Police planting drugs on African Americans and arresting them.

The continuing history of Human Rights violations goes all the way back to the worst Human Rights violation every the American system of slavery. Just as the Human Rights violations by the USA have continued since slavery so have the resistance of efforts of our people.

And we can't forget to mention the murder of African Americans by white civilians. The most horrific type of murder was lynching and riots after World War I despite African American soldiers dying to defend this slavery Posed society. Many nameless African Americans have died needlessly or for entertainment of white vigilantes and white civilians.

Now that this country has become more diverse with brown brothers and sisters from Mexico, the Caribbean, Asia and the Middle East many of the new comers have been killed by police, such as particularly

Mexicans and even African Haitians like the one who was assaulted by a stick and Momodu Diallo of Guinea, West Africa killed by NYPD in New York City where recently Eric Garner was choked to death.

I hope you can see that African Americans do not have a local, regional or state problem. In terms of the continuing violations of our Human Rights before and during the Obama Administration we have a nationwide national problem.

Death by chocking, like Eric Gardner occurred many times in the sixties, seventies and eighties so it was totally shocking to see brutal chocking was a factor or method in earlier times by clearly this has to be a law against using a choking as restraining method since It has resulted in deaths while in police/prison guard custody. We need a natal law against police/prison guard terror and brutality including a ban on chocking and shooting people in the back when suspect is known to be unarmed and not yet guilty of a capital offense.

I call on African American and other progressive lawyers of every ethnicity to come together and write a proposed legislation in time so that all presidential and legislative candidates can voice their opinions prior to the 2016 elections of this anti chocking anti police brutality, prison guard and vigilante murder as well as anti-state violence proposed legislation. Only truly national anti-state terror/violence-legislation could over rule the police bill of rights that unfairly favors police shielding them from being accountable for a ten day period. In the cases of the late Mike Brown and the late Freddie Gray led to a national shame and police murder without justice or justice delayed. Victims and families need prompt justice when their loved ones have been assassinated or injured by the police who are agents of the government and prison guards are agents of state.

As a former government teacher the issue of the continuing problem of police/prison guard brutality Human Rights violation is an undemocratic mess in America. It is a democratic shame. It is a disrespectful, racist throwback to slavery, and modern undemocratic Human Rights violation. I say Dump Trump, but I would not vote for any candidate for the 2016 Presidential Election if the candidate does not support national legislation to prevent police/prison brutality terror and murder. Truly Black lives matter however the continuing human rights violations indicate that police bill of right weigh more than African American human rights.

I say dump Trump because his record in my opinion, Donald Trump would be worst that the second Bush and even worst in terms of African American political interests even worse than racist Ronald Regan. I proudly say Dump Trump because he is the champion of the extremely rich one per centers who never allow progress in the USA. Trump and his one percent buddies are most responsible for the gross income disparity. I would never vote for Trump. I say dump Trump. Trump is the darling of the racist right ring whites. I say dump Trump for his insensitive remarks calling all Mexican immigrants "criminals" on national TV news programs. Trump is the great white hope but Trump is also the typical ugly American. Trump is an elitist and way too conservative for an American people increasingly Black, Brown laboring or working and immigrant based population. The demographic factors and the fact that although there are many white racist, the majority of young whites are progressive and non racist and hopefully these progressive will be a part of the new majority

But we can realize that however the struggle for self improvement and Black liberation is our responsibility primarily. However once we as a people come together as a solid united people we will find it easier to work with the progressives of every ethnicity including the old minority.

Many young whites will not see Donald Trump as the white savior that is scared of the new majority like old whites would be. So no matter what happens, I hope that everyone will pile on and dump Trump.

The conservatives/ Republicans will never admit they represent white supremacy and elite richest 1 percent political interests like the support for voter suppression that has an undemocratic manipulation robbing African Americans and other national minorities of their voting power. This group of conservatives' in particular championed slavery, 3/5ths compromise, the undemocratic Electoral College, dirty tricks that led to the murder of MLK And Malcolm X. Historically conservative racists said segregation yesterday, today and forever. So to me conservatives are undemocratic, scared of the new majority, justify the oppression of Blacks and other non whites and condone the excessive extra judicial murders especially of my people as collateral damage. These same people are responsible for murder of colonialism all over the world as well as the continuing exploitation of Africa and the rest of the underdeveloped world.

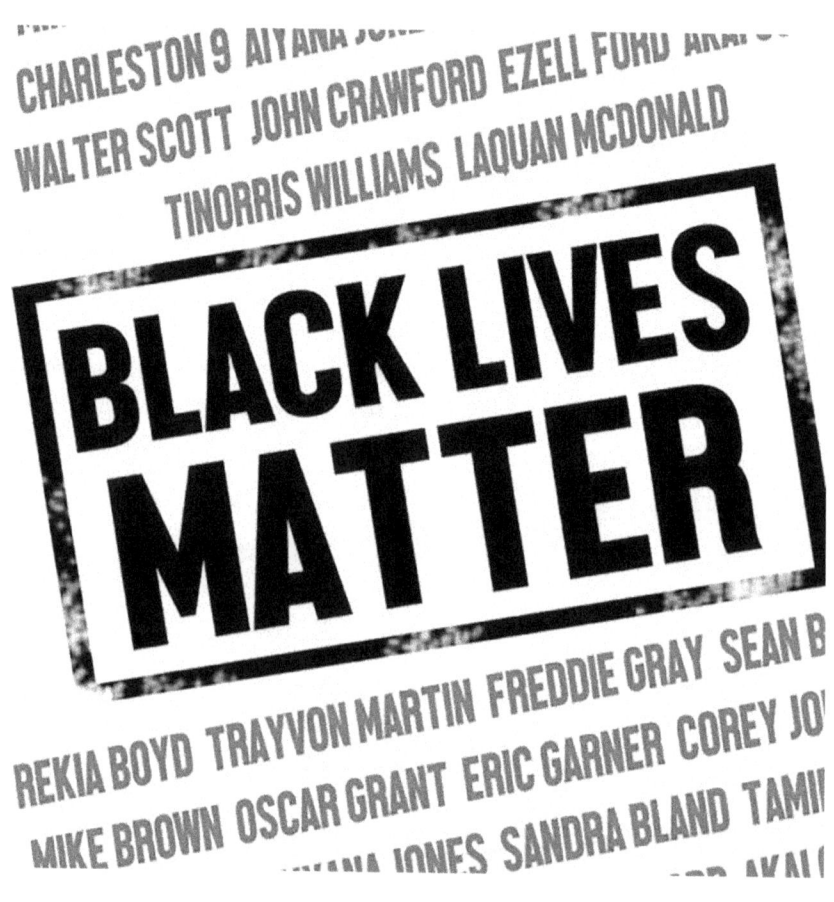

Reflections on Sandra Bland, here you have an activist sister involved in the "Black Lives Matter" movement who is aware of her rights and vocal about it. She get's stopped for the most minor traffic infraction that usually is overlooked by police when it involves white or civilians of any race who has a relative on the force. Next, she is beaten into the ground and we see the video in the racist state of Texas by sheriff deputies. Here is a public email I received from the late Sandra's sister Sharon.

Dear Larry,

My name is Sharon Cooper, and I am Sandra Bland's sister.

These past few months have been very difficult for my family. Since Sandra's death, we have been in mourning, but our ability to mourn has been paralyzed by the unusual and unsettling circumstances surrounding her death. That is why I am writing to you.

Our confidence in the local investigation to date has been shaken by numerous inconsistencies.[1] Our family has been given limited information about the case, while Waller County jailers have had unfettered access to the crime scene. Furthermore, local officials leading the investigation into her death have preexisting professional ties that highlight serious and concerning conflicts of interest. They have overtly tried to stain Sandra's name and four months later not one person has been held accountable.[2]

We need the Department of Justice to intervene. Will you join me and 85,000 ColorOfChange members in urging Attorney General Lynch to investigate Sandra's death?

My sister Sandra—affectionately known as Sandy—was a vibrant, outspoken, intelligent 28-year-old who was absolutely full of life. The circumstances surrounding her death are extraordinary, suspicious and unclear. Only Attorney General Lynch has the power to bring together the necessary resources we need to find the truth.

We need Attorney General Lynch to hear your voice. Please join my family and I in calling for a federal investigation into Sandra's death and the policies and practices that led to this tragedy.

Best regards,

Sharon

This beautiful confident young sister was murdered (hung southern style) in her cell. Of course she died in custody without a trial. How many times have African American Human Rights been violated in this way North or South, East or West? And she is put in a place without video. How many times has this happened to African American's I'll answer, it has happened for 400 hundred years in racist white American. May the late Sandra Bland, may you rest in power and peace.

The murder of Oscar Grant was the first murderer police to go to jail for killing a Black person but only for a number of months. Many of the other police and civilians murderers got away with it and think killing an African American is the thing to do and put notches on their guns and get promotions from their departments or the KKK or even both.

After a recent murder in South Carolina, cradle of the Southern Confederacy, a police was charged with murder after shooting an unarmed 54 year old brother and trying to plant his teaser on or around the dead body. The only thing this police was videotaped by a brave brother from the Dominican Republic. Most of the white racist civilians who kill Blacks from the late Emit Till to Eric Gardner to Mike Brown to Sandra Bland to Larry Lumpkin to Michael Black to Mathew Johnson get away with it and rarely spend a day in jail violating African American Human Rights. We need National Legislation to prevent the continued robbing us and others from their Human Rights well progressive lawyers where are you.

African American lawyers where are you and when will you get started or do we need more victims? Progressive African American lawyers when will write proposed national legislation that will be prepared to stop this murderous madness and police terror??????? Our lives do matter

One thing that needs to happen to increase the value of African American lives is the implementation of a Strategic National Black Consensus. What is the Strategic National Black Consensus?

Here is the Strategic National black Consensus, a follow up interview from a scholarly magazine and current commentary on new thoughts about implementing a Strategic National Black Consensus.

Here is the original proposed Strategic National Black Consensus reprinted from part 1 of this book

This piece Moving Towards A Strategic National Consensus is a reprint form Part 1 of this book and an interview with a magazine interview added along with additional comments

Moving Towards A Strategic
National Black Consensus

Moving towards a Strategic National Black Consensus as a framework for working together to improve our Economic, Academic, Cultural, Social and Political Interests. In short the more we move towards a positive mentality upgrade represented by moving towards a Strategic National Black Consensus, the more we internally empower ourselves to achieve our primary, secondary and tertiary political, social, academic cultural economic and political goals the more we will make progress toward liberating ourselves from oppression, depression, self destruction, white supremacy, Black on Black brutality and ultimately Black on Black killing. Study African- American History from Black Inventors to Black victims of lynching, 40 Acres and mule-Reparations to the difference between5/5ths and 3/5ths of a human being in the American constitution and know it!

Why is a consensus among the Blacks in the USA a necessity? In times past African-Americans depended wholly on leaders, however, the best way forward is for African-Americans to respect leaders and but also add more personal energy to resolve issues like the increasingly high incarceration rate, police brutality and other problems of African-American's and the Black on Black murder rate that we observe to be on the increase. This elevation of Black self hate resulting in an increasing number of deaths of primarily young Black men, our future!

For the potential of our young Black men's future that are failing school or being failed in greater numbers, we need to come to a broad consensus to accomplish several goals! We must also step up our efforts to educate our minds and learn to know better who our people are: African People all over the world. Reading this whole book is a great step forward in that positive direction of educating our mind!

The first or primary goal is to collectively say to young Black men—boys and young black women—girls, that we support you and want you to have every opportunity necessary to achieve success in school, and job or professional life or college/University!

The secondary goal of any broadly based nationally based strategic consensus must be to communicate to African-American jobless that we as a people prioritize their receiving job training, education, relevant education as well as a paying job for this most important segment of our population to put as many as possible back on a positive career path and paying jobs. Our tertiary or third broad goal must be to assist our people in the greatest numbers possible to avoid street fights and street wars among African- Americans primarily but also between African-Americans and other ethnic or racial groups so we can harness all of our energy for self improvement and self empowerment activities!

The last and most potent reason for a strategic National Black Consensus is to focus our population and the society in general on why reparations must be paid by the US Government to compensate for 400 years of slavery and oppression including the 3/5ths clause of the US Constitution.

In order to press in the most effective way for reparations, we must achieve a consensus of ideas, priorities and goals so we can move forward rapidly to achieve at levels of success a growing majority of our people can support this act of establishing a Strategic National Black Consensus is as important as a people the magna Carter was to the British people facing injustice from their 12 century king.

Strategic National and International Consensus among African People in the World

A Consensus of thought for African People all over the world is the first step from inappropriate powerlessness to appropriate empowerment.

Developing the United Black Empowerment Model on a worldwide basis should not have to be stated, however, in this our African World full of scattered Black Nations and Black/African populations, we should all begin to embrace development of an international consensus to eliminate Black on Black murder of all types all over the world.

In the book 'Loving Black Women', I made a call for on All African People's Congress to begin a World Wide African Conversation. Even though it has not yet happened on a scale envisioned this type of gathering continues to be vital and necessary as black kill other Blacks in Africa, America and in other areas while those with this broadly based thought of an International Strategic Black Consensus to halt acts of Black on Black violence and murder and focus our energies on working together and trading together to develop people to people social, economic, cultural, political and blood ties among our people! There are progressive conventions occurring all over the world like a Pan African Convention coming up this year (2016) in South Africa.

Once we achieve upgraded relationships in our local arenas among ourselves, we will be able to see the importance of the international component of our strategic International and National Black Consensus to assist our people in developing conscious more united outlook and a more united mentality or way of thinking to reduce the negativity of Black on Black self hate and Black on Black killing in all areas where we live in this world.

Once we have developed this united mentality and way of thinking, we will see the emergence of a United States of Africa, African People's Republic or other United African State or Entity. The full expression of an international Black Strategic Consensus would be the convening of a fully representative All African People's Congress made up of Africans from all over the world in Lagos, Nigeria or Accra Ghana outlined in more detail in my book Loving Black Women within an essay titled African World African Identity at the beginning of the book.

African-Americans Mexicans and Other Latinos/Latinas

All of the groups listed above include Black skinned people—among the Mexicans and other Latinos/Laminas are many Afro Mexicans in areas like Vera Cruz, Mexico, Honduras, Nicaragua, Brazil, Uruguay, Paraguay, Cuba and throughout the Spanish/Portuguese speaking world.

In the USA, these groups are often manipulated against each other particularly African Americans Mexicans and non gambling Native Americans. The manipulation only benefits white supremacy that harms us all!

The challenge these two populations face so heavily represented at the bottom of this society is for these two less empowered populations to see their political interests are best served by developing cooperation on a consensus of ideas and united practices of those developed ideas in the schools, communities, in the US Congress, and in the general US and Western Hemisphere as a whole!

We must note that in addition to the role Mexico plays hosting African populations of the Afro Mexicans, the US African-American slaves often escaped into Mexico and at that time freedom. When both of these oppressed populations see their common political interests the petty conflicts will end and the united action will proceed.

Ethnic Glue Among African-Americans

My main focus for writing this book is to generate new ideas on developing more Ethnic Glue for African-Americans who may be losing all Ethnic glue as we see more and more Black on Black violence and murder in our communities in the USA.

Still we also see the racism that produced the Jena 6 and the white oppression within the case of the SF-8 many of who are now freed from unjust charges! We also see the 50 bullets fired into innocent until proven guilty late Sean Bell in New York City. We see the rape assault and kidnapping of a Black Sister in West Virginia and other acts of white oppression in a white supremacy State in America.

Still with all of the white on Black and Black on Black violence can we maintain our ethnic glue as African-Americans? Ethnic glue and self-love are one and the same for African-Americans or Africans born in America and African People around the world.

We can but only if we consciously and purposely decide that we as a people will maintain our sense of ethnic glue and self love as a people.

We have to decide anew and again that we will keep our love for each other as a people in special part of our hearts and utilize that love-self love and love of our people as a motivation to end the Black on Black murder and violence that is on the rise among our people especially inside our communities.

We as a people must embrace our humanity as African-Americans and African People in America to show love for each other as a practice instead of self hate or we will make the term ethnic glue a useless term! African- American adults, children and youth should love each other, Africa and Africans with that special love!

We African-Americans have definite African Roots. This was really obvious to me when I lived in Nigeria West Africa for 4 years seeing African Men, African Women as well as African youth and children who looked just like us, identical to all types of African-Americans. However, sharing African roots with Africans and Africa leaves us in a zone of self-hate when we say we love only our American heritage and hate our African heritage. In that zone of self-hate we nurture anti Black sentiments that allow us to proceed down a path of a self-destruction!

Therefore, we must encourage our youth and young people to love Africa and Africans as a part of us African-Americans loving ourselves. We have to love our African self at least as much as we love our American selves as African-Americans to be balanced self-loving African People positively connected to other Africans all over the world and to be our whole self.

In a land disunited and dominated by white supremacy minded people symbolized by George Bush and the other neocons—Neo Conservatives who like the ones proceeding see America as wealth building and Empire Building while being at war with any plan or program that promises to assist African- Americans. These people would also be against African-Americans receiving just and proper reparations of

$1,000.00 to $500,000.00 for the middle passage and the 400 plus years of slavery and oppression.

In a land dominated by white supremacy where African-Americans are a minority although a substantial Black Nation, it may be a path to ignore one's own identity while over embracing the majority culture that is guided by white supremacy involving Willie Lynch style divide and conquer tactics to be deployed on African-Americans especially if they/we speak out about our many issues.

But can we calculate the costs of ignoring our identity to our people as a whole? We have the power to control our image once we realize how important it is for us to get along with each other better to empower each other.

Continuing the move towards a Strategic National Black Consensus.

We have to visualize ourselves as African-Americans in a multi-cultural world represented by populations from all over the world. We should practice tolerance and benefit from tolerance in equal measure!

However, we must embrace as many of us as possible a path to peace, progress, development, self improvement and unity or choose to continue down a path that includes Black on Black murder and crime, self-destruction, joblessness and a lack of self-improvement.

Between these two paths, we must individually consciously and hopefully collectively make the choice that will result in our people making as much progress as it is possible to make it in the white supremacy state until we are given justified reparations!

Remember our tax dollars paid for Japanese reparations - given to Japanese who are taken to concentration camps during World War II years. These wrongs must be made right in our case too.!

Each Japanese American who was interned or jailed for the World War 2 years was given a check for 20,000.00 during the Reagan Administration.

Until that time comes, we cannot allow ourselves to move towards self- destruction when the path to enhance our chances for success through a strategic national black consensus remains open to us a people. Please make the right decision my people?

Continuing the call for 8th and 9th African People's Congresses and Defining needed African-American preparations!

So we need to continue, and I continue, to make the call to have the 8th and 9th All African People's Congresses to empower our powerless people all over the world. We can go home thinking in and out of the box about ways to make progress.

However, on an individual basis, we as a people need to rebuild empowerment and embrace self love, ethnic glue, Black Unity, African Awareness more Black self love, less Black self hate until we embrace the path toward a strategic National Black Consensus including a more United State of mind and United Mentality so we can end Black on Black murder and violence and empower ourselves better! Once we are better to ourselves, we will find it easier to define our relationships with other groups, no matter their ethnicity. However self love like charity must begin at home!

Order your copy of American Challenges in the Obama Era Part 1 for only $2 .99 cents at this Amazon.com link to read this thoughtful book. http://www.amazon.com/s/ref=nb_sb_noss_2?url=search-alias%3Ddigital- text&field-keywords=larry%20ukali

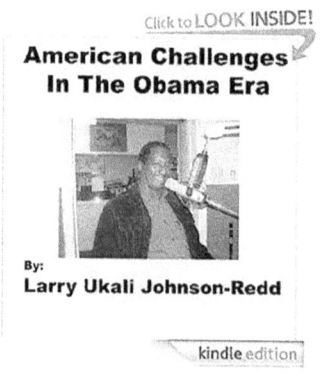

The interview in the Journal of Pan African Studies is what follows here:

When will a National Strategic Black Consensus be implemented? That is up to the activist African American, working African Americans and every day African Americans. To all of you, I ask this question because we need empowerment. And implementation of this proposed National Strategic Black Consensus is something only we can do after so many years of fighting and killing each other to entertain whites by force and during slavery and then continuing with this potentially genocidal behavior to fight for the white masters crumbs and dollars after chain or chattle or property slavery ended and half freedom began till nowadays.

Brothers and sisters we have a big job in discontinuing black on black violence and black on black murder as well as black on black crime. And we have to stop the violations of our Human Rights by militarized police inspired by white supremacy. That is our African American challenge. Challenges for the world Obama the US and the world and challenges for everyone in the world. As we move into the time that Obama is a lame duck President, we must note that although there is a current Black man president, we are still fighting for our Human Rights. And those who believe in white supremacy yesterday, today and tomorrow like the segregationist of the past remain in control of American business, government and this society. People like Donald Trump and his supporters, one per centers and the upper middle class continue to support the white supremacist locally and thought out the world. This factor gives the African Americans and people all over the world challenges. Obama spoke out emotionally after the death of Trayvon Martin after his death by a white vigilante but instead whites and police continued to kill us.

As I write in September 2015 it has been a rough couple of years so the work needs to keep on telling the USA diplomatic, government and people that USA should stop its current White Supremacy practice or remain like Donald Trump and the other conservative racists or remain the world's greatest hypocrites. You white supremacist cannot continue business as usual racial discrimination and police terror/

murder of African Americans without appearing like the biggest hypocrites in the world.

Meanwhile African Americans can support the International American Imperialism and the national white supremacy projected by 650 USA military bases in every area of the world. (Hopefully we should determine our own political interests and stop allowing White America and the Donald Trumps and like hawks to bully us. We should declare ourselves as against right wing intervention, colonialism, racism and white supremacy. We are in favor of National Liberation and reparations for African Americans as well as a strategic national black consensus. We also want to see the end of American imperialism so we may see and enjoy world peace.

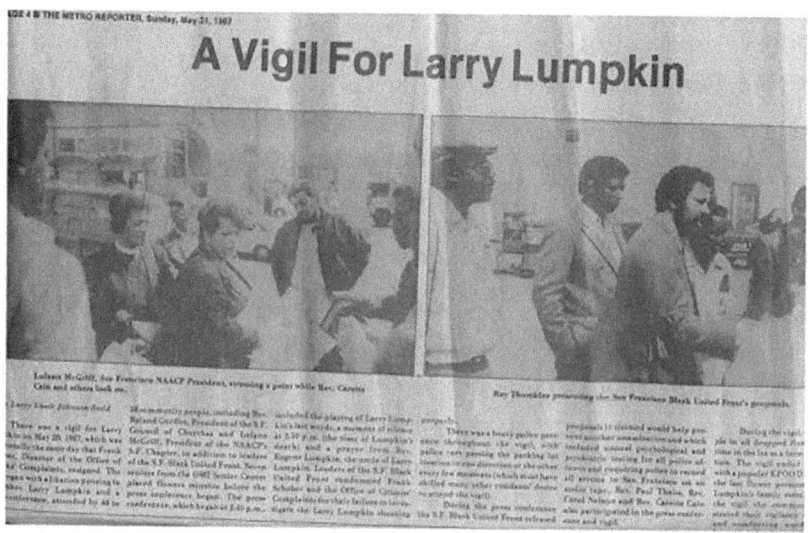

My memory of Larry Dean Lumpkin

I never met Larry Dean Lumpkin while he was alive however I still remember that when two prominent members of San Francisco Police Department on May 20, 1986, the time was between 4:00pm and 7:00pm. Larry Lumpkin was like many young brothers. Larry had done a little time. He was 24 years old. Larry needed a job. At the time I was President of the board of the Oceanview, Merced, Ingleside Pilgrim Community Center board of directors. The million dollar community center was under construction one block away on Arch and Randolph Streets in

San Francisco's Lakeview unofficially the street name because Lakeview was the street name however officially the area I lived in from o to 17 or 18 years old was called Ocean View Merced Heights Ingleside was a working class neighborhood where black people owned their own homes. However OMI was always known by African Americans throughout the city as Lakeview.

This city of San Francisco is where two white police corned Larry Dean Lumpkin in the Victoria Market parking lot between Russell Street to the left and Victoria Avenue, the parking lot is big at that time I was ¾ through build the much needed community center. Larry D. Lumpkin again was corned by two white men who never identified themselves according to witnesses never identified themselves. They were deep undercover their old car did not have a radio. So Larry

D. Lumpkin turned around after noticing the two white men with guns in the middle of the black community and tried to exit from an two unknown, unidentified white men and as soon as he was about he was shot in the back of the head many times. No ambulance was called and it took the coroner three hours to get his head out of his butt and show up. Meanwhile, Larry Lumpkin lay dead, assassinated in the parking lot on Randolph street lot.

A crowd gathered of hundreds of residents roped off by the police reinforcements that arrived. I was across the hill at the OMI Community Association on 201 Holloway Avenue in San Francisco, CA. writing foundation grants requests to seek funding for the new O.M I.-Pilgrim Community Center we were building within a block or two from the parking lot that Larry Lumpkin was assassinated in by two SFPD Police Officers while the new community was under construction. I had no radio or even a call during those three hours. Finally after three hours of bleeding and dying in a rental car of his sister Linda's friend the coroner finally arrived.

What I now remember was the two officers were never arrested and walked away due to their status as top brass sons of SFPD.

I also remember the esteemed Attorney John Burris was the family lawyer and Larry's Uncle was Reverend Eugene Lumpkin a Divisadero Street Pastor. Brother Larry Lumpkin's parents were given a small settlement amid the petitions and cries for justice. It might have been as little as $50,000, however, the mom died of a broken heart in one or two years and the dad also died within five years.

Aside from the small settlement no justice was ever served to the police killers. So now I offer my poetic memory, I wrote for Larry Lumpkin, a late dreaded brother who cut his hair so he could look for a job.

Fast forward to the present in the death of Trayvon Martin, he was assassinated by a vigilante named George Zimmerman. Very few vigilantes or police are ever held criminally accountable for killing black men or black women.

Many thought that when Obama entered the White House we would enter a post racial era however the murders of African Americans continued from slavery to lynching the murder of Emmet Till to Michael Black in the eighties a Black Boy playing with gun like the late Tamir Rice in Cleveland.

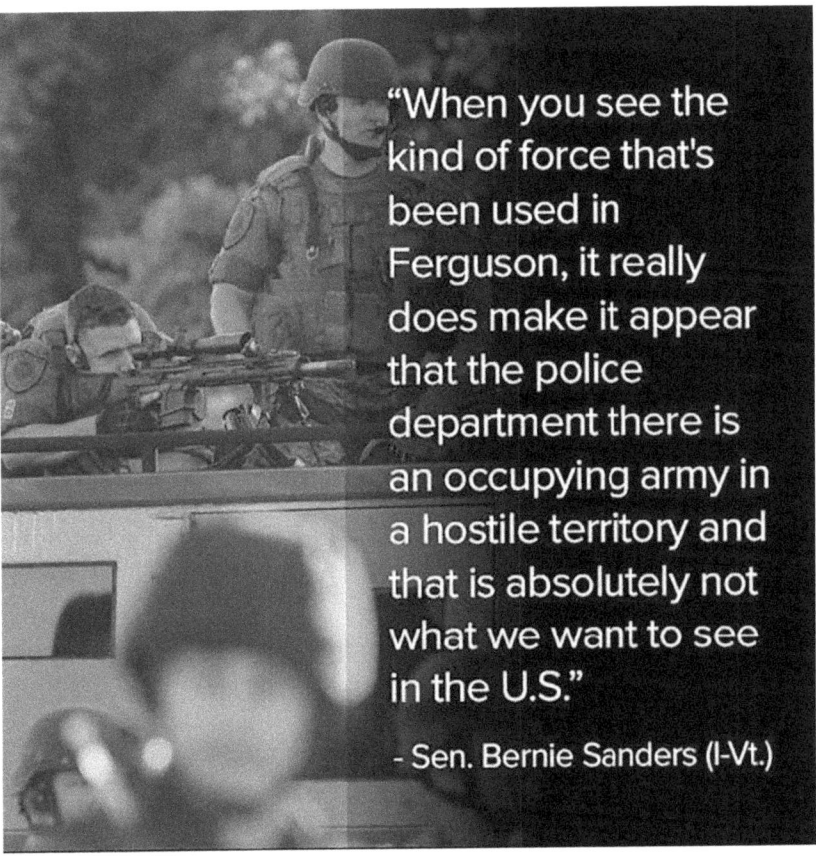

"When you see the kind of force that's been used in Ferguson, it really does make it appear that the police department there is an occupying army in a hostile territory and that is absolutely not what we want to see in the U.S."

- Sen. Bernie Sanders (I-Vt.)

Now we have police watch groups and even "Black Lives Matter" as well as New Black Panthers. Even though Obama spoke out loudly about the late Trayvon Martin it is generally felt that despite all of the police terror and murder from the late Mike Brown Ferguson MO. To the late Freddy Grey in Baltimore, to Eric Gardner who died in New York City, to Sandra Bland who was out right assaulted before killed in custody possibly have all been Human Rights abuse/murder, yet not one indictment from the weakest justice department under Obama.

This may be Obama's biggest weakness. Some of the Katrina police murderers have been held accountable but not enough however nothing less the new national legislation that over rules the police bill of rights and outlaws shooting convicted suspect in the back mistreating or killing of people while in police or Sheriff/prison guard custody. Whatever the legal *bar* of evidence or proof currently used by the justice department for civil or human right violations should also be lowered to a realistic level as a result of such national legislation or the justice department will remain irrelevant.

If the murders and violation continues to occur unabated then who will be surprised when murderous police meet their demise or destruction although that is not what I am advocating.

If 50 to 75% of African Americans started participating in our fight for justice instead of the 15 to 20% now then we could shut down some police departments/cities or states to obtain justice otherwise things only get out of control.

We need to continue mass protest but instead of 20 to 25% of us participating we need 75 to 90% of us showing up along with progressives of every other races in protest of the sizing American would once again be on trial before the media and the rest of the world for violating a African American and others human rights long enough to overcome the legitimacy of white supremacy and white racism. If our protest continues to only draw 20 to 25% of us then things could get out of control, however, if we have 50 to 80% of us protesting, there is a better chance of issues being resolved.

President Obama must be congratulated for reestablishing Diplomatic Relations with Cuba after a 50 year American economic boycott

Additional Challenges for Obama, American and the World

Although Obama despite some efforts has been weak on stopping the violations of African American Human Rights he has been somewhat in his signature health care law. I have benefited and so have many Americans of all backgrounds and races from <u>The Affordable Care Act</u> landed me in health care where I had to hustle my necessary meds.

However the conditions are not the same that Regan faced but Reagan gave amnesty to Cuban economic and political refugees, however looking forward to the New Majority era coming and 60 million Latinos/Mexican's who with 50 million African-Americans, other immigrants, progressive whites continue the new majority that may or may not succeed the Democratic party should be give amnesty. I mean amnesty for all current undocumented people leaving the next move to congress to ratify or modify the amnesty. I challenge Obama, if he has anything left or any principles left to give amnesty to the undocumented because that 12 million people and a civilized county could not deport ever 6 million without being charged with Nazi like Human Rights violations.

I also think Obama must fundamentally condemn the three deaths in custody, Eric Gardner, Freddy Gray and Sandra Bland. I ask Obama to consider pardoning African American Political prisoners from the dirty tricks era for the Hitler FBI era i.e. Marcus Garvey, the Louisiana Angola 40 years or more in custody and Abdul Jamal from Philly and all of the original Black

Panther political prisoners. Obama should also leave an executive order or memoir decreeing the murders of African-Americans and others killed by police and ordering new respect of African American Human Rights Obama needs to use his bully pulpit to continue police terror/murder while taking back the military gear sold or given to police because now there are massive amounts of violations of African Americans and others Human Rights, stifling of the rights of protest in Ferguson to Detroit and other places to come in the future should the police murder and terror against African Americans and Latino and others.

Challenges for All of America

As the so-called land of the free and home of the brave better characterized as the home of the slave from cradle to the grave, America voting in a black president was a good first step but unless you clean up the dirty tricks of the Hoover FBI, Nixon era and Bush's surveillance and police murder/white vigilanty murder of African Americans as well as the mass incarceration of African American men by letting them go free as well as reorienting the economy and country toward full employment this is Obama's challenge and America's challenge. America you must close many of the six hundred military bases and renounce previous views about claiming world domination that American has claimed since the end of World War II. America must reorient itself to full employment. American once for all end police prison guard brutality and murder. America you can't promote Human Rights around the world while violating African American and others Human Rights here in America. America you have the biggest challenges of all countries in the world or stay involved in external and internal world domination and risk collapsing from within, like ancient Rome!! America end private prisons and chain gangs. America has the highest incarceration rate per capita of all countries in the world.

Challenges to the rest of the world

Caribbean Region you need a uniquely Caribbean Strategic National Black Consensus and possibly a United States or United Republic of the Caribbean to unite the region and make sure that region no longer has Human Rights violations of any type so what is needed in uniting the power of people/workers of the region and provide full employment for the people of the Caribbean. This state will oppose Yankee or American imperialism, colonialism and white domination.

Many of the people leaving Africa, Arabs are leaving Syria because their lives are not livable. Western inspired or American and Western European supported wars and local reactions to those wars contribute to the pressures leading to the people leaving their homes in the Middle East and Africa as well as the Caribbean South and Central America, however African people have a bigger responsibility not to let the West, East, China, USA, Europe or any other combination of factors cause the amount of animosity and disunity harming the destiny of Africa.

There is a rich class in every African country and though I am writing from a long away my experience living in Africa leads me to now that in Nigeria there is a government reservation area where elite people live. The masses live in other areas. There is massive competition for jobs and unemployment among all sectors of the population because the I M F mob from the Western countries forced choices to privatize the economy instead of focusing African efforts on promoting a full employment economy.

The Caribbean if united would be stronger together however the Usa and Westen Euroope under present conditions would be the violent opposition. And that too must change to a policy endorsing world peace and liberation.

Africa needs a United States of Africa including all or most of the countries on Africa's main land and islands.

Africa needs a United States of Africa including all or most of the countries on Africa's main land and islands.

I am not the only person for recognize this need for a United States of Africa. Marcus Garvey of the UNIA to Kwame Nkrumah called for a United States of Africa. A United States of Africa developed as a full employment state will reverse the flow of African people suffering all types of atrocities to leave Africa to go to the West where they will face massive radical racial discrimination a problem worst that the problems that lead them to leave Africa. Racism and the privilege associated with white supremacy will sour many of the efforts of people risking their lives to leave Africa.

However many of the little African state and even the great state of Nigeria individually cannot control the American corporate exploiter so deeply involved in profit taking in every African third world country. Profit takers only want to keep Africa and Africans under the present arrangement to keep up the flow of profits.

Africans must unite among themselves, ourselves and develope a United African country including all willing states and African populations to develop a full employment state. If the opportunities exist at home 90% of those leaving African would stay.

This effort would have to come from within Africa and be supported by all Africans in the world. Once we show the dynamism to stand up for ourselves many of the profit taking exploiter corporations will get on board or pack up and leave Africa.

The time for a United States of Africa is now so as to have an independent future. However, many African elite may fear this type of change threatening their elite position. However, a new United States OF Africa focused on a full employment economy will offer massive opportunities for all Africans at home and abroad.

So I ask you my people of Africa and Africans all over the world let us continue the possibilities and liabilities of a United States of Africa to stem the flow of people leaving our Motherland. We also need to adopt a new strategy to being about African unity all over Africa that now is divided by foreign religions from the East and West.

We Africans must unite and develop a United States of Africa or Peoples Republic of Africa to employ our ultimate empowerment model. Somehow the West doesn't provide the correct development model because it is blinded by white racism and the operation of white supremacy. The Western countries including America want to dominate Africa. Bribe or pay off the current elites so they can continue to rape Africa of its resources. If these stolen resources stolen by western corporations and the USA were available to Africa as A WHOLE FOR IT'S DEVELOPMENT THOSE MIGRANTS DYING AT SEA WILL BE HOME IN Africa and well.

Africa must unite and form united government of its choosing or be swallowed up by the International Monetary Fund and Western corporations that are backed up by the American Military forces.

Africa we must finally unite and for a United States of Africa or People's Republic of Africa on all the mainland and islands of Africa. Let this African conversation continue brothers and sisters. We Africans and African Americans all over the world must stand up and fight for our rights while uniting among ourselves and eliminating poverty, Black on Black murder and Black on Black crime as well as white supremacy exploitation of the Western democracies like the USA and Western Europe.

United States of Melanesia

When white explorers found blacks in New Guinea, Vanuatu, Solomon Islands, Fuji and even Australia, they named the native Black people of the Melanesian region Melanesians instead of African to keep the Black peoples of the world divided on paper for exploitation purposes hoping we as African and Black people of the world never unite and put all of our dots, peoples and power together!

But we must unite as the Black Peoples of the world who are also victims of White Supremacy racial discrimination and economic exploitation. We as a people need to have a world forum to discuss our status and connect the dots. The internet is needed but we need more than that!

If empowerment is the objective then a United States of Melanesia or a People's Republic of Melanesia must be considered.

Melanesian Black People are also victims of White Supremacy, Black on Black murder, mayhem and exploitation of ugly American/European Corporate greed like Africans all over the world.

Also Melanesia remains occupied by Indonesia to the West particularly the Western provinces of the island of New Guinea and the power of the Indonesians. I begin the discussion however the people of Melanesians Island must be the deciders on this matter.

Unity for Empowerment? The People of Western New Guinea are fighting violently and politically to take their island out of the Indonesian governments control. How do we empower the region best to achieve Melanesian political objectives?

I would like to hear from Melanesians all over that region to understand better their regional points of view as part of the world wide African conversation and their analysis of USA president Barack Hussein Obama.

Black people all over the world have the ability to have the empowerment of a regional or in Africa's case an African National State or in the case of the Caribbean Islands. Empowerment efforts are best when smaller governments are being dominated by ugly American based profit taking corporations. This is the neo colonialism of this era. However an underpowered people gain power over their destiny by making into more powerful states to end neo western colonialism and even Eastern hegemony / domination and colonization.

The Obama Administration Challenges and the Challenges of America

This is about the Obama Administration but this book is also about the structure of American from its roots, its constitution, and its sad history of enslaving African Americans for hundreds of years. The American slave trade is the biggest, bloodiest most savage system in the history of the world despite the existence of a constitution. In many ways America because of its historical and contemporary white racism never really accepted President Obama like America would have accepted a white male or a white president. In Ferguson, Missouri highly militarized police/National Guard advance on crowds of protesting African-Americans and allies AFRTER THE MURDER OF Mike Mike Brown.

The constitution as it was written is a gross Human Rights violation like the kidnapping of Africans for slavery is a gigantic civil rights violation. In this country with its history of racism, Obama though brave, and a brilliant constitutional lawyer, did not even have a chance to be a great president or even to challenge the ever present foundation of white supremacy and white racism. However Obama stayed tight with party instead of the people who elected him. And for the record Obama as president failed to humanize African Americans to America despite pleading with American when Trayvon Martin was assassinated by a white minded ethnically mixed George Zimmerman. At that turn Obama said if he had a son he would have looked like Trayvon Martin. Even that gut wrenching admonition preceded two years where there have been a massive amount of USA police terror and executions including the assassination of Mike Brown in Ferguson, Mo. The murders of Freddy Gray and Sandra Bland while in government custody.

And the list of police murders continues!!!!!!!!!!!!!!!!!

and terror meaning beatings and bloody killings in African American communities qualify American as a democratic mess.

Let us look at America's Foundation

The Founding Fathers

Cyprus Attucks earned American citizenship for African Americans during the Boston Tea Party agitation. He was a free Black man but one of the first to die for AMERICAN democracy IN AN INCIDENT KNOWN AS The Boston Massacre , he was killed by British Loyalist troops during the American Revolution. Has it done us any good?

I have spoken to and read several American historians who say well you can't judge the founding fathers by current standards giving the founding fathers a pass on their racism despite Cyprus Attucks a black man and probably many others died for democracy acknowledging Africans fought on both sides Britain and American in the American Revolutionary War.

The British took Black in their losing army to Nova Scotia, Canada while a precious few African Americans continued to enjoy limited freedom in the North while in the South the enslavement of African Americans continued even while the constitution was developed and debated. Many of the founding fathers like George Washington and his Mt. Vernon Plantation and Thomas Jefferson the second US president had rape based relationship with the same African American women who they debated were not human. We were termed cattle, Niggers and 3/5 of a white human person even white they were mating and making children with the women they held in bondage. So the founding fathers should not get a pass foe their white supremacy racism because their hypocrisy betrayed Cyprus Attucks and hundreds of thousands even millions of African Americans.

America's first constitution could have freed African Americans however that was America's second betrayal of African Americans civil political and Human Rights.

The third American betrayal caused the American Civil War. Had white America learned by the time of the Civil War shortly after during the reconstruction period ended in the 19870's where white America compromised away Black freedom paid for in the blood of African Americans shed along with white and federal soldiers were withdrawn so white citizens/vigilantes/former slave masters continued to deny our civil and Human Rights as well as human and economic rights until 1965 when the Voting Rights Act took effect. Between 1870 and 1965 thousands were lynched, shot, houses and businesses were burned down just because bold African Americans registered to vote. A poll tax was instituted to stop only African Americans from voting. The Scottsboro boys were tried on phony charges. Black freedom fighter

Marcus Garvey was framed by the dirty tricks of J. Edgar Hoover who was even rumored to be gay however Hoover and the FBI held intelligence on American Presidents from the 20's to the 1960's as well as directing dirty tricks against African American leaders from Marcus Garvey to Martin Luther King. With all of this killing of African Americans and dirty tricks going on against the Black Panthers and any brave Black man who spoke this was another betrayal and broken promises to our African American's dream of freedom.

But did all the oppression end with the Obama Administration? Although African Americans would or could blame President Obama as commander in chief for the police terror and political voters' suppression and racial discrimination that has continued.

Typified by the police murder of Mike Brown, Eric Gardner, Freddie Gray (whose family has been awarded six million dollars recently) Trayvon Martin killed by a vigilante and hundreds of other African Americans like Larry Lumpkin, Sandra Bland, Mathew Johnson and Oscar Grant have continued to be killed by the police and in most cases police get away with it and little to no accountability has occurred.

Against the history of racist white supremacy American President Obama has probably tried his best but white capitalist racist corporate America has continued to to harass and kill and oppress African Americans that despite Obama's best efforts our, Human Rights remain incomplete and that countries like China still call America on that hypocrisy and not a democracy.

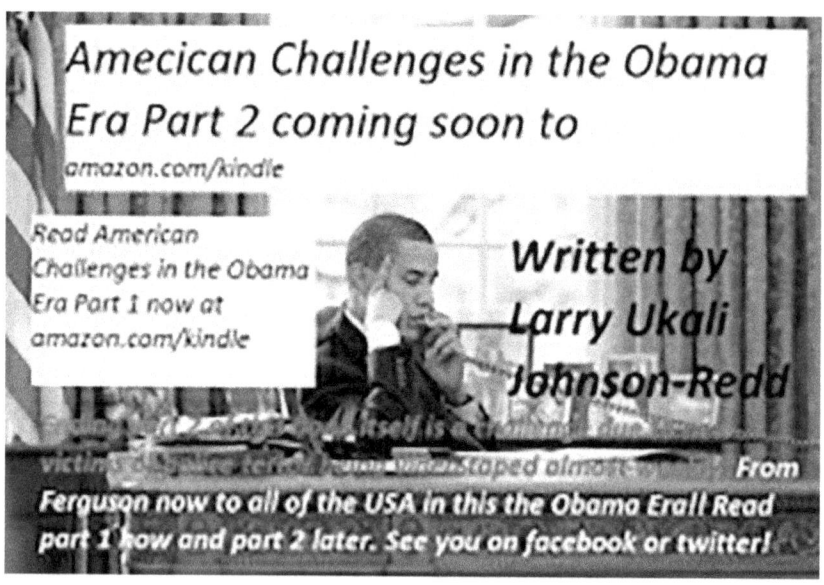

America's challenge in face of its failures to respect African America's Human Rights should free African American, Native American, Porto Rican political prisoners like Mumia Abu Jamal, The Black Panthers, Leonard Peltier as well as the Louisiana-Angola 3-all three. After freeing political prisoners, America must dismantle chain gangs and prison labor exploitation.

The prison industrial complex and the military industrial complex must be dismembered. People convicted of victimless crimes should be released as soon as possible and America must reorient its economy to full employment economy to provide jobs for the millions of unemployed. Oh while I am at it any country that attempted to deport 12 million people including many refugees would be in the similar company with Nazi Germany. So the 12 million current undocumented must be given their amnesty and freedom and if President Obama started by giving out the amnesty, he would claim his place in history as well as earn the love and respect of Mexicans ,Mexican Americans and Latinos and Latinas as well as other immigrants.

Personal Appeal to President Obama

President Obama give amnesty to political prisoners of all races and amnesty to undocumented as your last act or even right now. And I dare White America and its ugly white supremacy to try to reverse progress again because if changes do not occur we may go from a melting pot to a cauldron of fire and political oppression. President Obama your health care act saved me but there are still millions without medical insurance, but, please free political prisoners and give amnesty to the 12 million undocumented! However, America's greatest challenge is to end the mass incarceration of young and old Black men.

More Commentary on Current Events

A YouTube video of Stockton, California policeman beating on a teen who was at a bus stop occurred exists. In the video you see a young African- American after being beaten by a long baton being used and trying to protect his precious head. Then the policeman calls for help. Seven or eight officers arrive and they bring the youngster down as a group.

The reason it goes viral is the excessive force that would not be used on a white teen. Racism and police terror are again way out of control. The teen was charged with trespassing and resisting arrest. How can you be trespassing at a bus stop? Another trumped up charge. If Donald Trump wins we'll see more of it but Obama by himself cannot stop it.

We as a people will need to unite and commit to protect the Human Rights of people. Like the old days, 70 to 75% of us need to attend rallies for Human Rights like the 50's and 60's. We must demonstrate again these attacks against our Human Rights in much greater numbers to be effective.

Well the Pope is coming to American however the challenge remains. Although the Pope from Argentina wants to visit with and raise the profile of the homeless and the poor he also wants to make a scene. I won't call him father because of his use of force to capture and so call "civilize" the Native Americans. I am not in favor of oppression of Native populations by the force of the church and the military. Stand up Native people! Racism is Racism.

Donald Trump—Now Trump in the second Republican Party debate states a man who says Obama is a Muslim and a non-citizen. Trump is a bither to remember. He laughs as this right wing idiot continues insulting all Muslims by saying all are America's enemies. Then ask Trump what you would do about it. Dump Trump because Obama showed his Hawaii birth certificate to shut Donald Trump and his brothers. Trump acted totally racist by not challenging his supporters. Donald Trump must never be US President.

Trump also says if president he would ban Muslim immigration.

The Immigrants/ Refugees from
US Military Wars for Resources—Oil

Immigrants by the hundreds of thousands walking through Europe to Germany mostly Syrians, who are in a way: refugees from the invasion of Iraq by Bush 2 and the USA military. Many of the millions of refugees are Africans. Countries like Hungary show a lack of compassion. So does most of Eastern Europe along the trail -refugees travel and among the war refugees are Sudanese and Nigerian and people from other Middle East refugees from Afghanistan. However all of this commotion is rooted the 500 years of American and Western Europe's colonialism and manipulation of the Middle East and Africa to take oil and other natural resources for profits for Western Corporations in the resistance to these profit taking efforts.

International Law allows for the free movement of refugees especially war refugees but these Human Rights are also being violated in Southern Europe. If the West led by the profit motive would stop raping the world of natural resources and halted the western military intervention in Africa and Asia as well as the Middle East, we could begin to see world peace. Ethiopians and Eritreans are among the refugees pointing out the need for a United States of Africa will be nation building continent wide in Africa to lower the flow from Africa of economic and political refugees.

Profit driven global intervention or full Employment and the end of the mass incarceration of the military, Industrial Complex and the Police/ Prison Guard Industrial Complex are the broad alternatives. "Black Lives Matter" has approached several 2016 presidential campaigns. So far on Mr. Barney Sanders from Vermont among all presidential candidates has addressed police terror and USA world intervention. So far the others supported by profit motives have promised no changes.

Once again our experience with the Obama Administration is that a change at the White House doesn't change conditions on the ground with continuing police terror for non-white communities.

However, Donald Trump is the king of the ugly Americans, racists and interventionists and profit driven idiots. Even the progressive from Vermont or like Obama may run from the left and govern from the center protecting profit seekers, however progressive people everywhere must stand up, mobilize and change conditions on their political turf to make sure that profit driven intervention ends and full employment and Human Rights begin, so we can overcome police terror as the primary interaction between the people especially Black as well as Brown people and the arms of government in the USA.

The conservatives/ Republicans will never admit they represent white supremacy and the elite richest 1 percent political interests like the support for voter suppression that has a undemocratic manipulation robbing African Americans and other national minorities of their voting power. This group of conservatives in particular championed slavery, 3/5ths compromise, the undemocratic electoral college, dirty tricks that led to the murder of MLK And Malcolm X historically.

Historically conservative racists said segregation yesterday, today and forever. So to me conservatives are undemocratic, scared of the new majority, justify the oppression of Blacks and other non whites and condone the excessive extra judicial murders especially of my people Black People as collateral damage. These same people are responsible for murder of colonialism all over the world as well as the continuing exploitation of Africa and the rest of the underdeveloped world.

BLACK UNITY MATTERS

Black Love Spoken Word ll

I'm a poet
From the sixties
I can flow it
From the seventies and eighties

From the nineties
Times to the present
You should listen
And your time is well spent

We were closer to freedom
In the sixties
Many of us treated each other better
Like sister and brothers

Stood together
And fought for our rights
We had many issues to fight
From the KKK and whites on the right

Now we beefing
Among our selves
How we going to get along
So we can get strong

They look at how
We disrespect and kill each other
And wonder if
We are sister and brother

How are we going to get along?
With anyone else
When we can't get along
With and among our self

Consider this, sisters and brothers
If we can't get along with each other
How will we get along?
With all the others

Try to be right by each other
Then things will get much better
Get our voting rights back
From voter suppression others

Could we join progressive others
Out every other race
When the way we treat each other
Is a total and a sad disgrace

How can we enjoy rap
If it s all about threatening each other
Couldn't we rap about how?
Treating each other like sister and brother

This is to celebrate the past times
This is the present in my rhymes
It should blow your mind
How we killing our own kind

How can we advance beating?
The Conservative voters suppressing others
If we cannot do right
By each other sister and brother

This is real time
Walk this walk
This is real talk
Walk this walk

Aren't we weary?
Of a war against ourselves
Burying our young people is hell
Sons and daughters in the cell

Time we better to each other
And treat each other again
like sister and brother
cause we are stronger together

This is Black Love Spoken Word ll

Make It Good

Make it good
In the hood
Have pride
In our neighborhood

Show self esteem
For a sister queen
Why shoot a sister
Why be so mean

It is our
Responsibility
To treat each other right
In tha hood keep it tight

In a liberation fight
We can not win
Unless we treat
Each other right

Stand up please
as a people off your knees
We got to make it good
For our people in tha hood

Don't shoot
a brother
Don't shoot
Another

Make it good
In our hood
You know we
Really should

You know
You could
Make it good
If you would in tha hood

Start a truce
Cease all fire
Black on Black peace
Is our People's desire

Don't shoot your
brother's head
cause he wears blue
or he wears red

Put you sites
on fighting for our rights
Economically you know
We hang like kites

Our hood needs
Economic development
You and I need more help
from each other and the government

No More Deadly Wakamo

Give a brother
a real job
So we have
Have to rob

In Hayward, Richmond
And Frisco too
No deadly Wakomo
No brother no

It was our labor
that built this land
Together we can
Re Build Oakland

Avoid 1 step forward
And 2 steps back
We can do better
Brother that's a fact

We don't need
Every other day
Another brother short
Hear what I say

No brother No
Let the violence go
We can do
So much more

No more deadly
Wakomo
No brother No
No Brother No

No Brother No
Don't play
Deadly Wakomo
With you brother
No brother No

When you
Shoot a brother
You shoot
A brother's mother

And the
family too
and
You kill you

No more
Wakomo
End that flow
No brother No

In deep
East Oakland to Berkeley
My brothers and sisters
In all flat lands

Partner homicide
Is Black Genocide
Together we can
Build Black Pride

We must
say it
We know it's true
It is up to you and me

In North Oakland
And West Oakland too
In East Oakland
You know its true

Give a brother
a real job
So no need
to rob

In Hayward, Richmond
And Frisco too
No deadly Wakomo
No brother no

It was our labor
that built this land
Together we can
Re Build Oakland

Avoid 1 step forward
And 2 steps back
We can do better
Brother that's a fact

I HAVE NOT FORGOTTEN SANDRA
I HAVE NOT FORGOTTEN TAMIR
I HAVE NOT FORGOTTEN MICHAEL
I HAVE NOT FORGOTTEN ERIC
I HAVE NOT FORGOTTEN TRAYVON

I have not forgot Mario Woods

Let A Sister Be Praised

Let a sister
Be raised
Let a sister
be praised

Not just noting
Oppression
This a positive
Expression

From the ash heap
Of white history
To the queendom
Of African History

From the segregation
Of the white nation
To the top of
Our African Nation

Let a sister
Be raised
Let a sister
Be praised

She is our diamond
In the rough
She survived so beautiful
Our sister is rough

She is our
Treasure chest

She is unique
And she is the best

Through abuse
And scorn
From us our
Sister was torn

Cause she is
Special to us
I am
Serious

Let those who dare
To keep a sister down
Find a way
To rise from the ground

Lift our sister up
Lift her image too
Sisters you know
We need you

Don't put our sister down
In your city or town
Don't be a fool
Cause sisters are cool

Let a sister
Be raised
Let a sister
Be praised!

Message to online friends

Hello to all of my Face Book Friends and others, (Please read all 4 e-books friends.) I Larry Ukali Johnson-Redd wish you all a happy weekend and I ask you for you to buy one or all of my E-books Loving Black Women, American Challenges In The Obama Era Part 1 and my memoir Long Distance Love, Loving Black Women and History To Destiny, Through Afrocentric Poetry. I also have a 170 paged paperback titled Journey To The Motherland, From San Francisco To Benin City. All of my books are available at Amazon.com/kindle.

Many people are buying Kindle and other types of reading electronic units like Ipad, Ipod and I phones for e-books. You can also buy my e-books on your Black Berry phones and even your computers as we move toward a paperless society. Please give me your support and use the link I included or go to Amazon.com and click on Kindle books in the Department pull down, Now put my name in the search and you will see all 6 of my e-Books.

http://www.amazon.com/s/ref=nb_sb_noss_1?url=search-alias%3Ddigital- text&field-keywords=johnson-redd&x=18&y=22

Why Do We

Why Do we got
To threaten each other
Why can't we
Be sister and brother

Why can't we
Work things out
Then we would all
Have more clout

Why can't we threaten?
Each other
Why can't we
Be sister and brother

Why do we
Fight each other
Why can't we
Love each other

We are discounted
By some others
We are profiled
Like no others

But since the
Beginning of time
When we are fine
Everything is fine

Why do we
Got to threaten each other
Why do we
Threaten each other

Why do we people
Threaten each other
Why can't we all
Get it together

Why do we
Got to issue a threat
Deadly violence
We all regret

Why can't we
Just get along
Why do we
Treat each other wrong

Why?????????

Chicago Black Graduates by way of the Black Star Project

So Fine

So fine, So Fine
Black Woman you
I think about you
All the time

So fine, so fine
Hear me today
Hear what I say
You are so fine

In the rain
Or sunshine
Black Woman of mine
You are so fine

You look good,
Smart and fine
I wish you were
All mine

So fine and fine
You are a good find
You are so fine
I wish you were all mine

Where Is My Own Very Special Queen

I see my sisters
On the BART
I see my sisters
on the bus
Can you tell me
One thing
Where is my
Sister queen
I see my sister
In the street
In the office
And in the suite
I see you
On your feet
A good sister
Can be so sweet
I see my sister
In the church
Tell me one thing
Where is my special Queen?
I see you
On TV sometimes
I see you
Smile at me
I see you
In the city
I see you
in the country
I see you
Standing in line
My special queen

You are so fine
I can see
I'm not blind
My special queen
You I must find!
Is that you?
Over there?
I do love
Your hair
Is she, a pretty Queen?
With all the self esteem
That is an important thing
To this tall king
Is she very nice
With brains
Brown Sugar
And spice
Will I think
Of her once
And then
Think twice
With a knowledge
of our history
And a sense
of mystery
That wants a 1 on 1 with only me
Where in the world
Is my special Queen
For this Man and king
Pretty nose, pretty eyes
Pretty Legs, Pretty thighs
Pretty face, pretty lips
Pretty skin, pretty hips
Over here,
Brain sense

What is Fratricide?

What is?
Fratricide?
Another Brother
Just died

You know
His people cried
Killed by gun
The night he died

Fratricide
when brother kills
brother

Fractricide
When brother
Kills sister

What is
Fracticide
In face of
Genocide

When we
Need to stay alive
If we die
Will we thrive?

And their people
Still cry
Years after
Their young die

What is
our fate
Increasing the
Death rate?

Act like
You know
Close
that door

Let our
Poverty
Be about
Money?

Not the
Poverty
Of our mind
But the future of our kind

What is fratricide, homicide, genocide
What is Afrocide?
Who cried?
Who died?
W hat is fratricide?

IF WE'RE
FIGHTING
EACH OTHER
WE CAN'T
FIGHT THE
ENEMY.

See It Soon

Making Martyrs
Is our doom!
May we see
May we see it soon

Not just for
A tune
Another one falls
As bullets fly zoom zoom

When we could
Wear our throne
Shooting through
A brother's dome?

A realization
Must surely come
Can we realize
What has been done

Black Death
Is an ugly tune
Black Destiny
May we see it soon

Open our eye
Regain our pride
Black Folks unite
And watch us rise

Can we see
A brighter day
Can we sort it
Out a better way

Self-genocide
Fratricide
Let Black Love
Help us survive

When eyes are dried
When we find our pride
When we unite
We will thrive

May we open!
Our eyes
So we
Can rise

Shooting each other
Is our doom!
OPEN OUR EYES
AND SEE IT SOON

5.0 out of 5 stars Great job again by L.U.J.R.!!! American Challenges In The Obama Era Part 1. March 3, 2013
By T-Mo

American Challenges In The Obama Era Part 1 is another hit for long time author Larry Ukali Johnson-Redd. I am a long time fan of his work. He is consistent and writes beyond fluff in favor of getting to the core for his readers. I recommend his book. As an 8-time Best Poet/Performer award winner and author of 17 books myself, I'd like to say I know good poetry when I read it. I have each and every book Larry has written and appreciate his talent to the max point.

I really like the poem Obamaland and the breakdown of liberation in the Obama era. This book mixes serious educational writing with strong but delicate around the edge poetry. Good job! I learned a little something. It has a lot of deep information and positive suggestions for our Government. A call to action is what I get from this book. This book should be very useable in schools regarding African American study subjects. Very profound!!

Terry Moore aka T-Mo

American Challenges in The Obama Era Part 1,a thought filled Kindle e- book is available at amazon.com at the link below and costs $.99. Use your Ipad, Ipod, Kindle or any other media. In order you read my e-books on you desktop please download the free Kindle app. Part 2 of this book is in progress.

http://www.amazon.com/American-Challenges-Obama-Part- ebook/dp/B003Y74QP6/ref=sr_1_5?ie=UTF8&qid=1362634387&sr=8-5&keywords=Larry+Ukali+Johnson-redd

Journey to the Motherland from San Francisco to Benin City e-book by Larry Ukali johnson-Redd availabe at amazon.com/kindle. Look at Lagos, Nigeria and then order my e-book and as you read, we will travel all over Nigeria. Also read my other e-book based in Nigeria called Long Distance Love Africa for Africans at home and abroad

Till, Evers, Grant and Martin 2013

Emit Till, Medgar Evers, Oscar Grant
Trayvon Benjamin Martin
A Black has no right
Any one or white must respect

Instead of killing
Each other or disrespect
It's ourselves we
We must protect

The non Black Jury
Let Zimmerman go free
Not even 1 Black person
Was allowed on the jury

29 year old Zimmerman
Killed 17 year old Trayvon
The fight stated with racial profiling
Then Zimmerman fired his gun

While Trayvon lay there
Zimmerman shot him dead
After that maybe Zimmerman
Scratched his own head

Till was killed
And Evers too
Then Oscar Grant
Now Trayvon too

And where does it stop
They still call us Coon
Will we have to rise up
For it to stop soon

And brothers kill brothers
Morning, noon and nights,
Remember we still got to
Fight for our rights

Trayvon Martin
Iced Tea and Skittles candy
Trayvon committed no crime
Zimmerman free and all is fine

End non Black juries
Or face our fury
If Trayvon killed George
He would never walk free

When a Black kills a White
Execution is the norn
When they kill us
The guilty are never found

Through an all white jury
We are always guilty
When they kill us
They always go free

So much for the post
Post racial society
Kill a Black Minor
And you are not guilty

We still remember Oscar Grant
Assassinated on the BART Platform
Racism and Profiling
Has caused this storm

Too many more
We can't name them all
Racism and profiling
Makes our brothers fall

Victims of the state
We must hear the call
United we stand
Divided we fall

Black Romance

Written by Larry Ukali Johnson-Redd 12-30, 2011

Black Romance
For African Americans and Africans
Black Romance
Nothing to do with Romans

Black Romance
For strong Black kings
Black Romance

For beautiful Black Queens

Black Romance
May it never ever die
Black Romance
Don't make a sister or brother cry

Black Romance
Don't let it rust
Black Romance
Always between us

Black Romance
Fly like a black Dove
Black Romance
Full of beautiful Black love

Black Romance
Never bought or sold
From our heart to
Our very soul

Black Romance
Oh so tenderly
Black Romance
Sweet as it could be

Black Romance
With every tender touch
Black Romance
It means so much

Black Romance
In our community
Black Romance
Keep it as sweet as it can be

Black Romance
Respect should be
Black Romance
The only way for we

Black Romance
One on One
Black Romance
May the joy come

Black Romance
May we advance
Black Romance
Love and happiness

Black Romance
Make it fun
Black Romance
Until the morning sun

Black Romance
For you and me
Black Romance
Sweet as it can be

From her lips
To her pretty nose
Black Romance
For your Black Rose.

Peace In The Hood

By Larry Ukali Johnson-Redd

Peace in the hood and
It's all good
Love in the hood
It's all good

Stadiums of Black Bodies
From Black on Black Crime
And Black on Black survival
On the line

Black on Black crime
Is disempowerment
WHAT WE NEED IS
Unity and empowerment

Fill up the stadiums
For Black empowerment
It's Black on Black crime
We must prevent in this time

We are losing
More than those lost
This war against ourselves
Has a bloody and deadly cost

None of our eyes
Should be dry
Black on Black violence
We must ask ourselves why

From the HiFi east
To the Bottoms West
Can't be saved
By a bullet proof vest

Drive By shooting
On a young brother
With young child
Black in Black Crime
Murder gone wild

The Ku Klux Klan giving out metals
For self hating shooters
The KKK are
Black on Black crime boosters.

If there is
peace in the hood
Brothers
it is all good

Too many drive by's
Done from cars
We are losing too many
From Black on Black wars

Why you want to stand
In another brother's blood
Black on Black crime
Makes no sense in this time

Until there is a slow down or
A truce on Black on Black crime
There will be Black on Black crime funerals
All of the time

This is not a just a rhyme
Stop Black on Black crime
So we African Americans
Can rise and shine

Zimmerman killed Trayvon Martin
We know that is true
Black on Black crime
Threatens me and you

If there is
peace in the hood
Brothers,
it is all good

Too many drive by's
Done from cars
We are losing too many
From Black on Black wars

Why you want to stand
In another brother's blood
Black on Black crime
Makes no sense in this time

Until there is a slow down or
A truce on Black on Black crime
There will be Black on Black crime funerals
All of the time

This is not a just a rhyme
Stop Black on Black crime
So we African Americans
Can rise and shine

Follow this link and hear this piece Trayvon Martin Memory-live-in an interview with Sister La Teta on Blogtalkradio.com or go to you Tube where I have 28 clips including this piece.

http://www.blogtalkradio.com/sister-lateta/2012/04/29/common-sense-common-knowledge-and-accountability#.T6HvZgQYrQM.facebook

Trayvon Martin Memory
By Larry Ukali Johnson-Redd

When I have a
Trayvon Martin memory
About a brother
Killed by a vigilante

I think of the
Killerman
Named George
Zimmerman

Then I think
Of our history
And the memory
of American slavery

I salute young
Trayvon Martin now Dead
by raising the hoodie
upon my head

I wish the young Brother
was not dead
while our people
are underfed

Zimmerman
Can't escape
Trayvon's life
He did take

And restitution
He can not make
To me George's
tears are fake

What a
racial tragedy
Profiling
You and me

Since the days
of slavery
We demand justice
In this racist tragedy

No bail,
Keep George In Jail
Cause Trayvon had a right
to live and a contribution to give

And peace to
The Trayvon Martin family
I pray for their healing
in this tragedy

Please support
The Martin family
Demand justice
Immediately

—

Justice delayed
is justice denied
Don't rest
Til Zimmerman is tried

No justice no peace
North or south
West or
East

Trayvon may your soul
Go to god whole
May you fly away to Africa
Like our ancestors of old

To Trayvon Martin
We pour libation
From peace loving people all over the world
And around this nation

The Beauty of a Woman Part 2
—Part 1 is in my book Loving Black Woman

The most beautiful scene
When there is real love shared between
Walking together
Commoners or king and Queen

There is instinct
In her DNA
And so much more
From her soul, her inner core

A woman can
Work her mojo
From her head
To her toe

Acknowledge her
Inner spiritual core
Give her respect
She may open every door

The beauty of a woman
Is the intelligence
In her essence
And her common sense

Her beauty is
Undeniable
That makes every man
Potentially pliable

While too many men
Are focusing on her
Body, thighs or butt
But let me tell you what's up

A woman's real treasure
You will wisely find
Is her spirit soul
Heart and mind

The beauty of a woman
If the story is told,
Hot or cold
is In her soul

Integrity
Makes a woman
Have beauty
You see

It's her integrity
Fused with her beauty
that makes her
a real cutie

And integrity
Can you see!
Behold, behold
Is in her soul

The Obama Administration 2013

Many are proud
Many don't care
Conditions on the ground
Are still not fair

Racial profiling
Some progress
Is white America
Trying its best

While stock markets
Are subsidized
By the Obama Administration
People still face massive unemployment

Tea party people have Cadillac
Health care while
Fighting implementation
Of Affordable health care

African American male's unemployment rate
More than double White unemployment rate
Let the poor eat cake?
Is this progress or fake?

Refugees from slavery and
The old economy
Unemployed in
The new economy

Is this progress?
Does it pass the smell test?
Is this the same old mess
Or is this progress?

Police are not under attack, institutionalized racism is. Removing sexually abusive priests is not an attack on Catholicism, nor is removing ineffective teachers an attack on education.

o.com/GirlDuJou

Bad apples, bad training, and bad officials who blindly protect them, are the enemy. And any institution worth saving should want to eliminate them, too.

—Kareem Abdul-Jabbar

Splendor of the people

The splendor
Of a people
Is best expressed
When they are equal

No restriction
on our mothers in reality
No racial profiling
No racist police brutality

We can be good
To ourselves and society
When we are treated Right
And our rights are reality

Stop telling our people and
Empty out the jails
Give us our rights
Or all else fails

Get paid while
You are job training
Get money in the pocket
Sunshine a raining

Respect goes both ways
My people need freedom days
We can change some of our ways
To emerge from this phase

U.S.A. make societal change
End world domination on the world stage
U.S.A. end discrimination
Especially against the black Nation

We won't go away
We are here to stay
We demand social change
Release our people from this cage

Give is all our rights
So we can end all our fights/ rap
Give us what we need
And there will be no income gap

We want to see
The best of us
We need to see too
The best of you

We want of this country
Thus it is true
So don't act like you
don't know what to do

Bring on our best days
All boats will rise
And racial profiling
And we'll be smiling

Tribute to Nelson Mandela

Today they buried
Nelson Mandela
In Qunu, Transkei
South Africa

The highest tribute today
Hear me, I say
We need a Madiba today
All over America, No play

We need an
Indian Mandela
We need a
A Chinese Mandela

We need a
Native American Mandela
We need a
free Mandela

We need a White Nelson Mandela
We need a Black Mandela
We need an Asian Mandela
We need an Arab Mandela

We need an Israeli Mandela
We need another African Mandela
We need a Brown Mandela
We need a Polynesian Mandela

Madiba the reconciler
A reconciler is greater
To bring the world together
And ban racial oppression forever

To end the oppression
Of all human kind
To the best way
A Mandela Council can find

Hello Brothers and Sisters in New York
City and the EAST COAST. PLEASE READ
AMERICAN CHALLENGES IN THE
OBAMA ERA PART1 including
Strategic National Security Consensus
this e-book on the
AMAZON.COM/KINDLE this e-book
written by Victor Emanuel Hoang

END STOP AND FRISK

End "Stop and Frisk"
We have a right to exist
America does not need
Racial Profiling like this

The practice by any name
Internationally it is a shame
We know racism is to blame
It's a racist undemocratic dirty game

From Stop and frisk
Racist police brutality in the midst
All across America police stop
Black and Brown men harassed by the cop

It is a democratic mess
Is a racist tactic full of ugliness!
White criminals go free
While police concentrate on you and me

End "stop and frisk"
The Racist enforcement mentality
This is more than a racist flaw
END THIS RACIST LAW

INCOME INEQUALITY and THE RICHEST 1%

There is a need
For Equal Opportunity
Upward mobility
Throughout this society

This stalled
Economy
Is bad for you
And for me

We are preparing
For upward mobility
Our obstacle is
racism in society

We face declining
Opportunities
Bush and friends
Outsourced many

of our jobs
away yesterday
and the economy
is stalled today

as the rich
get richer
the poor
get poorer

Income inequality
A one percent
Reality
Redlining and declining

When we must better
Could be done
With progress
For everyone

Stimulus for
Higher ups in the stock market
Through 2014
The one percent get everything

Stimulus for
The people ended
My friend
In the year 2010

Too few haves
Too many have-nots
The rich don't care
And poverty sucks

In equality
And unemployment
Increasing the promotion of hate
In this declining state

What will do
Me and you
This is what
Oppresses us through and through

Income equality
And widespread poverty
Income inequality is
The Shame of this society

History To Destiny

Through Afrocentric Poetry

By Larry Ukali Johnson-Redd

My people, My People

We can be a bigger figure
Don't call a brother a trigger
Take a look around
The 'N' word is a putdown

My people, My People
Don't call a bro a trigger
Don't kill a bro and
feed the grave digger

My people, My People
Don't call sis a b
or a trigger
when we could be bigger

My people, My people
We are still unequal
My People, My People
May we soon be empowered and equal

My People, My People
Try our best
We must unite
to pass the test

There was a time
we were called a trigger
We turned it around to
A term of love to make us bigger

My people, My People
We are queens and kings
Don't call us trigger
We are much bigger

We can not continue
To feed the grave digger
First stop calling
each other trigger

My People, My People
We feed the grave digger
When we kill each other
Because we devalue a trigger

My people, My People
Don't call each other trigger
My People, My People
Time we become bigger!

WE CHARGE GENOCIDE

Police Terror homicide
Police terror unjustified
We have been oppressed 500 hundred years
We charge genocide

Police brutality widespread
Many of us underfed
Sandra Bland is dead
Real African Americans seeing red

Police attacking Black youth
Tell our youth the real truth
The death of Freddie Gray was homicide
Systematic homicide, We CHARGE GENOCIDE

White Citizens council and KKK
A Stockton police hit a black teen's head yesterday
As he waited for a bus
Police abuse kills trust

A history full of excessive force
A messy democracy off course
The USA democracy
Police terror makes it a hypocrisy

The killings from Mike Brown
To Emit Till are homicide
We all must charge
The USA and the west with Genocide

Thousands of Police/Vigilante assassinations
A poor state of liberation
Sean Bell shot 50 times: he died
We charge Genocide

End the prison industrial complex
End police/prison guard complex
End police/prison racist text
We don't see serve and protect

Police/prison guard homicide
How can we thrive?
America outlaws our hope and pride
We Chare Genocide

End unequal heavy enforcement
In our Black Community only
Use equal enforcement
Throughout society

Because we charge
White society with
Practicing genocide on
Black society

End stop and frisk
Of Black and brown men
End srelect5ive enforcement
By police and the government

End racial profiling
Of Black and Brown men
The American people
Need enforcement that is equal

The founding fathers lied
The said only 3/5ths of a man
Our ancestors fought, cried and died
We Charge Genocide

To pay for genocide
Pay reparations not more homicide
Our ancestors hung like kites
While we still fight for our human rights

WE CHARGDE GENOCIDE

DONALD TRUMP IS A RACIST CHUMP

Donald Trump
Is a RACIST chump
We all must dump
Donald Trump

He says he will
Humanely deport 11 million
He is a moron
He is a racist scum

He hates the undocumented
Especially Mexico
He wants to build a fence
Don't you know?

We know racism
We've seen it before
We don't want racism
Never—any more

He is an ugly
American
White old days supremacy
Is his policy

1% wealth
Wanna Be
99% people's
rich enemy

Let the poor
Eat cake
Poor people
He is a fake

Worst than Reagan
Racist to his core
For his class and brand
Making a racist stand

Donald Trump
Is a Chump
We all must Dump
Donald Trump

Kiss your rump,
Donald Trump
We all must dump
Racist Donald Trump

NEW MAJORITY

What do you
Mean a new majority
The old majority
Was old, white and right.

What is the new
Majority
And its Priority
And the new policy.

What is the policy
Of this new majority
Who is going to enjoy
this American Society?

Is there room
For all of us
Or will there be
Deportation camps

Deportation camps
Like refugee camps
Like concentration camps.
Like Human or Prison Camps

Three strikes In California
Locking away
The heart of the—*New majority
In misery we can see

Is this a post
Racial society

Held back by
A racist minority?

Where are the jobs
for the new majority.
Where is the Black Community
Going to build its economy?

Where will old power concede
Where will the poor feed
Where will the one percent breed
How long will the new majority bleed?

Free young brothers and
sisters in prison camps
Or the new majority will
Break up the brutal/ financial deal.

Black, Brown
Red and Yellow
Among us we must
Keep it mellow.

That progressive white
He is a good fellow
Many immigrants
And people of color

America remains threatened
By our Black skin
For too many Blacks
Our skin in a prison

There is a population
Shift can you see
Coloring of America
With a new Majority

Who will represent
This new majority?
How will we make
Everyone feel free?

And the Black Community
Would ban police brutality
Remember Brother Rodney King
They beat him like he was a thing,

And what does the new economy
Mean for the Black Community
Faced with massive unemployment
And not enough help from government.

And for those in the
Inner City down and gritty
From LA to the City of Philly
The old majority had no pity.

Can we reclaim
Our outsourced jobs
Bring them back—a job
For those unemployed

Meanwhile in Chicago
The new murder capital
Can the murder rate this is my call
Can wee see a great fall?

Can we freeze?
The deportations
Of immigrant families
Please, please, please.

In the interest of
The new majority
Can we secure the borders
And give an amnesty.

Not to is so nasty
A racist brutality
Against the undocumented
And their family.

The challenges of the new majority
are a reality to you and me.
Deportation! A crime
When a family
Lacks a dime
Racist deportation is a state crime

If we are unemployed
Brown or Black or new majority
Tell those corporations this fact:
To bring our outsourced jobs back.

RACIST ACTS

May my words
stand tall!
May the oppressors
All Fall.

Where is
The grace
For the oppressed
Of every race?

Who is oppressing?
Who is downpressing?
Dropping bombs
And Shooting rounds?

Who is ailing?
Who is Jailing?
Who is jailing
Who is bailing?

Who benefits?
By the worlds oppression
The status quo in
A state of depression.

As many search
To make ends meet
Oppressors press
The low with their feet.

What will
Be done for the
Oppressed
Black One?

Victims of
50 Bullets
The Brutes
Are Unfit

And what will
A great Black
One Do
For those that society screw?

Help the Inner Cities
With jobs and social services
With jobs, Job training
And job placement we deserve.

And stop the
Racist acts
Of police brutality
Against Blacks.

And then you
Will really be
A Great Black One
Save an African American Destiny

Bring about
Justice and peace
Throughout the North
South, West and East.

End dreams of
World Domination
Prepare for
World Liberation.

So we can teach
The truth to the youth
And Harvest
Righteous Fruit.

Laws are needed
To stop Blacks
From receiving
Bullets in their backs

Stemming the power
Of the military, oil and sex.
The Prison, War Machine
Industrial Complex

Perpetrating
The poison of
World domination
Instead of World Liberation

We are ravaged
from being
Collateral damage
Treated like we are savage

Were your ancestors
Three Fifths of a Human Being
Could you describe?
This awkward feeling

Great Black One
When the right time come
Let justice be your great beacon
Link up and fight for freedom

And what
Will change do
In our community
For those that society screw?

What about
The homeless
What about
The hopeless?

And those in need
Of the inspirational seed
And those shut down
Surviving in the town.

There is also
Much to be done
To remove the Funk and Frown
Of those society holds down.

Let this journey begin
With a Civilian Job Corp
And paid Job Training
And provide the homeless
A real home

Thank you readers for buying and reading my books Journey to the Motherland $2.99. Long Distance Love$4.49. History To Destiny$2.99. Loving Black Women $2.99 and American Challenges In the Obama Era Part I $2.99 all available at Amazon.com/kindle.

Larry Ukali Johnson-redd
I completed writing the first draft of part 2 of my Obama book

Mobile Uploads · Sep 13 ·
Tag Photo   View Full Size   Make Profile Picture
Edit Photo   Send as Message

👍 Like   💬 Comment   ↗ Share

You, **Azahara Carter** and **2 others** like this.

Write a comment...   Post

☺   📷

(Summer Time Beat)
Most Beautiful Thing

A MOST Beautiful Thing
I saw a Black Queen
I heard bells ring
It was a scene

She was magnificent
A one woman scene
There was a greeting of
A queen by the King.

She had a lock
On the beauty thing
As she walked
Even the birds would sing.

Her smile was brighter
Than real bling, bling
But she surprised me

When she hugged the Black King,
Her lips shined
Her hips rolled
She was very hot

And very bold
A hot soul
It was a bright sunny day
She was not going my way

Tell me please
What could I say?
I remember that queen
Til this very day.

Dedicated to the late Ruby Dee and the late Maya Angelo

THE AMERICAN POLICE AND PRISON GUARDS

Poh Poh when you come to
Our neighborhood
End Human Rights Violations
And it's all good

You better know
Just how we're feeling about
Government supported
Unnecessary killing Police

End stop and frisk
And cuffing too tight the wrist
stop shooting us first
Like killing is you thirst.

An unnecessary
police beating
you better know
You are cheating

Act like you do in your neighborhood
In our neighborhood and it's all good
Don't violate our constitutional Human Rights
Because that is the basis of all our fights

Hostility to police/ prison guards terror
Will not end over night
In modern America
Its not right

You Poh Poh are challenged to make it right
You can't shoot unarmed suspects not in
Any neighborhood in the back
And it's all good

Excessive force and killing
Uncponvict4ed innocent
Is police and prison guard terror
Causing our families horror.

End racist texts
Give us our respect
Don't forget your job
To serve and protect.

THE HISTORY OF POLICE BRUTALITY

Who was the first slave catcher
the white slave master was the first kidnapper.
Then came 1865
It was hard to stay alive
With the lynching and killing
How could we thrive?

Many were hanged or burned alive
Slave catchers became police
Black Folks trying to survive
Now we in the City

With Slave hating
Slave catcher Police
Often disrespecting
You and Me.

The names of
The new victims
Continue to expand
Police killing Black
Woman and Black Man.

1967 Mathew Johnson
Killed by sfpd sparking the
Hunters Point Rebellion
Instability

1979 Sister Ruth Love
Sister Ruth Love from Los Angeles
In our history Police brutality
Killed by LAPD

Now Freddie Gray and Mike Brown are added to the list
Of those shot down
Eric Gardner was chocked and held down
We must stand up
The courage must be found

Now Sandra Bland was removed from the land
Beaten into the dirt
A real woman
Beaten like a man

Dying in custody.
Police Brutality
Stop and Frisk, Policing
Stop Human Rights Violating: stereotyping us,

From San Francisco to New York,
From Atlanta to Seattle
Police respect our Human Rights
Stop Murdering suspects

And hanging us like kites
Prison Guards Stop
Police Terror
In the Black and whole community

Stop Police Murder/terror
Human Rights Violations:

Dedicated to the late Mike Brown, Freddie Gray, Sandra Bland as well as Trayvon Martin, Mario Woods and all other victims of USA Human Rights Violations.

WALK WITH YOU SWAG

To the Young Brothers

Who got Swag?
Don't let a Threat
Be your drag
No Brag, keep your Swag.

Walk with your Unity
Among our brethren
Walk in Unity
With our Sisteryn

Walk with your Swag
With the Human Lives
As a Black and Proud Man
Say it quietly or loud

No Killing each other
No bluffing each other
Reduce the violence
Between each other

Don't be a killer of a brother
Respect every other
It's good sometimes to brag
And walk with you Swag.

Black August Memory

From 450 years
To 1971 yet our freedom struggle
We have made progress
Yet our freedom must be a success

Black August Memory
of government murder and brutality
at Attica near NYC
too many killed and injured are we free

And late strong Geogre Jackson
And they locked him on a minor robbery
Threw away the key
Black August Memory

They assassinated both
A Black Prince and younger Brother
George and Jonathan Jackson
Killed in an August Reality Memory

We remain hopeful
But can Obama make the change
End the murder / brutality of the state
Pardon the victims of Cointelpro FBI dirty tricks
And our un-free August Memory

Indeterminate
Sentence worst than 3strikes
For strong George Jackson they
Threw away the key
for a minor robbery

This is the Black August tragedy
That began this August Memory
And my brothers killed at Attica
Fighting to be free

And Grand old Marcus Garvey
And the UNIA
United States of Africa
Black August Memory

Marcus Garvey wanted empowerment
For disempowed us, so we can be free
August 17th his birthday
Black August Memory

This piece is all middle passage survivors past, present and future.

NEW MAJORITY

What do you
Mean a new majority
The old majority
Was old white and right.

What is the new
Majority
And its Priority
Amid at the new majority.

What is the policy
Of this new majority
Who is going to enjoy
this American Society?

Is there room
For all of us
Or will there be
Deportation camps

Deportation camps
Like refugee camps
Like concentration camps.
Like Human or Prison Camps

Three strikes In California
Locking away
The heart of the—*New majority
In misery we can see

Is this a post
Racial society

Held back by
A racist minority?

Where are the jobs
for the new majority.
Where is the Black Community
Going to build its economy?

Where will old power concede
Where will the poor feed
Where will the one percent breed
How long will the new majority bleed?

Free young brothers and
sisters in prison camps
Or the new majority will
Break up the brutal/ financial deal.

Black, Brown
Red and Yellow
Among us we must
Keep it mellow.

That progressive white
He is a food fellow
Many immigrate
And people of color

America remains threatened
By our Black skin
For too many Blacks
Our skin in a prison

There is a population
Shift can you see
Coloring of America
With a new Majority

Who will represent
This new majority?
How will we make
Everyone feel free?

And the Black Community
Would ban police brutality
Remember Brother Rodney King
They beat him like he was a thing,

And what does the new economy
Mean for the Black Community
Faced with massive unemployment
And not enough help from government.

And for those in the
Inner City down and gritty
From LA to the City of Philly
The old majority had no pity.

Can we reclaim
Our outsourced jobs
Bring them back—a job
For those unemployed>

Meanwhile in Chicago
The new murder capital
Cut the murder rate this is my call
Can we see a great fall?

Can we freeze
The deportations
Of immigrant families
Please, please, please.

In the interest of
The new majority
Can we secure the borders
And give an amnesty.

Not to is so nasty
A racist brutality
Against the undocumented
And their family.

The challenges of the new majority
are a reality to you and me.
Deportation! A crime
When a family Lacks a dime
Racist deportation is a state crime

If we are unemployed
Brown or Black
Tell those corporations
To bring our outsourced jobs back.

Racist Acts

May my words
stand tall
May the oppressors
All Fall.

Where is
The grace
For the oppressed
Of every race?

Who is oppressing?
Who is down pressing?
Dropping bombs
And Shooting rounds?

Who is ailing?
Who is Jailing?
Who is jailing
Who is bailing?

Who benefits?
By the worlds oppression
Status quo in
A state of depression.

As many search
To make ends meet
Oppressors press
The low with their feet.

What will
Be done for the
Oppressed
Black One?

Victims of
50 Bullets
The Brutes
Are Unfit

And what will
A great Black
One Do
For those society screw?

Help the Inner Cities
With jobs and social services
With jobs, Job training
And job placement we deserve.

And stop the
Racist acts
Of police brutality
Against Blacks

And then you
Will really be
A Great Black One
Save an African American Destiny

Bring about
Justice and peace
Throughout the North
South, West and East.

End dreams of
World Domination
Prepare for
World Liberation.

So we can teach
The truth to the youth
And Harvest
Righteous Fruit.

Laws are needed
To stop Blacks
From receiving
Bullets in their backs

Stemming the power
Of the military, oil and sex.
The Prison, War Machine
Industrial Complex

Perpetrating
The poison of
World domination
Instead of World Liberation

We are ravaged
from being
Collateral damage
Treated like we are savage

Were your ancestors
Three Fifths of a Human Being
Could you describe?
This awkward feeling

Great Black One
When the right time come
Let justice be your great beacon.

And what
Will change do
In our community
For those society screw?

What about
The homeless
What about
The hopeless?

And those in need
Of the inspirational seed
And those shut down
Surviving in the town.

There is also
Much to be done
To remove the Funk and Frown
Of those society holds down.

Let this journey begin
With a Civilian Job Corp
And paid Job Training
And provide the homeless
A real home

THE AMERICAN POLICE
AND PRISON GUARDS

Poh Poh when you come to
Our neighborhood
End Human Rights Violations
And it's all good

You better know
Just how we're feeling about
Government supported
Unnecessary killing Police

End stop and frisk
And cuffing too tight the wrist
stop shooting us first
Like killing is you thirst.

An unnecessary
police beating
you better know
You are cheating

Act like you doin your neighborhood
In our neighborhood and it's all good
Don't violate our constitutional Human Rights
Because that is the basis of all our fights

Hostility to police prison guards terror
Will not end over night
In modern America
Its not right

You Poh Poh are challenged to make it right
You can't shoot unarmed suspects not in
Any neighborhood in the back
And it's all good

Excessive force and killing
Uncponvict4ed innocent
Is police and prison guard terror
Causing our families horror.

End racist texts
Give us our respect
Don't forget you job
To serve and protect.

Read Journey to the Motherland

Understand this Lagos skyline- by L. Ukali Johnson-Redd @amazon.com

THE HISTORY OF POLICE BRUTALITY

Who was the first slave catcher
the white slave master was the first kidnapper.
Then came 1865
It was hard to stay alive
With the lynching and killing
How could we thrive?

Many were hanged or burned alive
Slave catchers became police
Black Folks trying to survive
Now we in the City

With Slave hating
Slave catcher Police
Often disrespecting
You and Me.

The names of
The new victims
Continue to expand
Police killing Black
Woman and Black Man.

1967 Mathew Johnson
Killed by SFPD sparking the
Hunters Point Rebellion
Instability

1979 Sister Ruth Love
Sister Ruth Love from Los Angeles
In our history Police brutality
Killed by LAPD

Now Freddie Gray and Mike Brown are added to the list
Of those shot down
Eric Gardner was chocked and held down
We must stand up
The courage must be found

Now Sandra Bland was removed from the land
Beaten into the dirt
A real woman
Beaten like a man
Dying in custody.
Police Brutality
Stop and Frisk, Policing
Stop Human Rights Violating: stereotyping us,

From San Francisco to New York,
From Atlanta to Seattle
Police respect our Human Rights
Stop Murdering suspects

And hanging us like kites
Prison Guards Stop
Police Terror
In the Black and whole community

Stop Police terror Murder
Human Rights Violations:

Dedicated to the late Mike Brown, Freddie Gray, Sandra Bland as well as Trayvon Martin and Mario Woods, Tamir Rice and all other victims of USA Human Rights Violations.

Final Thoughts
American Challenges in the Obama Era Part 2

I wonder what our African American Ancestors would say about slave owners 3/5th compromise in the American Constitution and the modern day slave master descendants and 1 % wealthy Americans many who said segregation today, tomorrow and forever still involved in voter suppression efforts aimed at stealing African American voting power as well as the voting power of other legal voters who are maybe not born again republicans. They can be compared to Hitler or worst planning how to wickedly deport 11 million people from all over this country who happen to be from south of the border. African Americans know if they do it to other non-whites, they will even be more harmful in atrocities to African Americans. Donald Trump is KKK approved and represents the continuation of White Supremacy and White Privilege of the old white majority. We may need a whole new constitution after hundreds of years of constitutional injustice.

I know our ancestors wanted to be free 4 or 500 years ago. And we African Americans should join with efforts to halt or stop or prevent deportations of our Mexican/Latino brothers and sisters. However we as African Americans must discover and rediscover ways to be kinder and better to each other now and in the future. We are a major group in the new majority however we will not be fully empowered until we are able to treat each other better whether we are being oppressed by the wicked and racist sector of white society or not. I hope the Black President on his way out of office will give amnesty to the Undocumented who have children here and who build up the USA everyday by their hard work and sweat like our African descendants built up America during and after slavery up to the present day.

The USA founding fathers were hypocrites ignoring the humanity of the African People they kidnapped, bought and stole while compromising with the plantation system, north and south in the 3/5th 's notions that it took 5 African Americans to equal the humanity of 3 Whites. The Electoral College is another Whites only compromise with Hamilton and many slave masters who feared real majority rule -democracy based on one person/ one vote. Most White historians give these so called founding fathers a pass on the hypocrisy and obvious white racism on their own white superior attitude. However what makes Jefferson and Washington and the founding fathers and white slave owners hypocrites and fake is while maintain the whites only racist slave system and legalizing slavery in the USA constitution, they raped and brutalized our African American sisters at while making babies with our sisters at will from the big house to the slave quarters. This is why the USA is like it is today. That pattern of white racism and white privilege has even shown itself to be even stronger that the African American President producing the ongoing white police racism and brutality to we see all across America that has been a constant during the Barack Obama Second Term.

I firmly believe that the new majority will one day rule America much more fairly than this old white majority constitution and government. I ALSO FIRMLY BELIEVE THAT America can only even the playing field for African Americans and the undocumented after AMERICA-ADMITS IT'S RACIAL SINS past and present IN A VERY PUBLIC WAY to African Americans and the world. But also America must pay Reparation's to the descendants of the people they kidnapped from Africa and forced to build America while depriving our descendants citizenship and the precious right to vote for 4 to 5 hundreds of years up to and beyond the 1965 Voting rights Act. White Supremacy continues to be a total threat to African American Human Rights.

HIP-HOP
4 BLACK
UNITY

Tell the Truth: America and the World
More Challenges for those who live in America

Maybe we victims of American racism and exploitation expected too much from the first African American president in what was then the coming of the Obama Era. After all America and Europe practiced a particularly wicked form of racist property or chattel slavery and colonialism on Africa, Asia, the Middle East and Latin /Central/ South America for 500 years. Maybe we expected too much from the Obama Era and President Obama with the historical white power structure and many working and upper class whites enraged by this first African American president. Another factor is America in particular, white America continues to be in denial of its racist history and doesn't really care about the victims of 500 years of racism and slavery. There are and always has been a smaller less influential group of whites like Bernie Sanders and even historically John Brown of Harpers Ferry fame. But this group has little power in terms of a comparison with the forces of white racism and exploitation like Wall Street, business elites the gun lobby and other white racists.

There is no excuse for denial of American's racist past and present. However upon the election of Obama and the beginning of the Obama Era we- many us speculated that maybe America had reached the status of a post racial society. However with all of the racism still intact in America nearly 8 years after Obama became President, Humans Rights violations of African Americans continue with police and prison guards committing murder and getting away with it and America particularly white America still in denial.

There have been and probably will continue to be bloody white interventions in the world anytime a non white population or leader rises up against the ruling white world in favor of ending the exploitation and racism of colonialism in their country. The leader is usually assassinated first and if that does not work then next is bloody intervention as well as denial. When the Congo rose up under Patrice Lumumba's leadership, he Lumumba was assassinated. In Haiti the leader was faced 2 American inspired military coups along with western denial. This racist colonialism is the basis of the Jewish occupation of Palestine and i.e. its policy of no state for the real people- of Palestine. And most times white racist forces choose to form oppositions to do their dirty work like the Haitian Military or in the case of the late Lumumba it was another Congolese named Mobutu.

This white racism and colonialism if we see and count all the dots is also the basis for the denial of Human Rights of African Americans, Native Americans, Asian Americans, Muslim Americans and Arab Americans as well as Latino/Latinas and Mexican Americans. And this is happening in a society under the cover of being the most modern country in the world. It is these oppressed groups united with the real white progressives offer hope for America's arrival at the post racial society if these groups unite to form the New Majority. It is only the emergence of this new majority that can change the dynamics of the savage white racism that has ruled America for 400 years. Donald Trump and his supporters want to keep it like it is or go back 50 to 100 years and keep white racism and exploitation in control i.e. White Supremacy.

The lynching's and killings such as the late Emit Till and countless other African Americans of the past are now replaced with the murders by police of Freedy Gray and Sandra Bland on video or secluded or in custody. These murders will continue in the future to disempowed victimized people and national minorities particularly African Americans until a new majority takes over America and the Donald Trump and other white supremacists are disempowered by the power of the new majority.

Reparations

America even at this late date amidst the rage they have built up during 500 years of racial oppression can right it's ship following simple civilized rules like repairing the damage with repair-ations paid directly to the present day descendents of the middle passage surviving Africans who are the foundation of African Americans or Africans in America. Secondly America can pay every African American $100,000.00 if they survive until 21 years old in the racist system in current AMERICA FOR PAST AND PRESENT CRIMES. But also America MUST RETRAIN OPPRESSIVE POLICE ACROSS THIS

RACIST COUNTRY. America must write up new rules of engagement or police polices giving more weight to human rights and the right to be tried after a supposed crime than police rights.

If African Americans saw Black Movement organizations in every state and region including Civil Rights organizations discussing and developiong a strong Strategic National Black Consensus and operational unity, African Americans generally would support a Strategic National Black Concensus and could use that energy to dramitically lower the rate of Black on BLACK BRUTALITY AND BLACK ON BLACK disrespect as well as Black on Black Crime. If we are united we have a much better chance of defeating White Supremacy and winning Black Liberation with the support of progressives from every part of the population inthe USA

Justice for Mario Woods
by Larry Ukali Johnson-Redd

I am so proud to be from the real San Francisco like the old Lakeview. Hunters Point and I lived all over Fillmore. We have always resisted oppression from SFPD. Back in Hunters Point, 1966 or so as a young boy, I looked at the Hunters Point Rebellion after SFPD poh-poh assassinated Melvin Johnson, shooting the brother in his head. That murder all by itself began the Hunters Point rebellion along with the massive oppression of our people by the government, police and society. Many on the east coast misread San Francisco. In San Francisco then there was the murder of Larry Lumpkin in Lakeview's Victoria Market by 2 police again shot the late Larry Lumpkin in the back of the head in unjust circumstances causing emotional heart ache. the SFPD murders of Larry Lumpkin never ware arrested despite many community members stepping to the Police Commission many times, circulating Petitions and Attorney John Burris represented the Lumpkin s family and a coalition emerged called the San Francisco Black United Front. There has been more oppression of San Francisco Black Community despite the city's liberal image. Now a newer younger and stronger coalition has emerged with 1 leader named Brother Salessi has emerged as a leader, I hear on KPFA FM Radio with the Bay Area Police Terror Network and Black Lives Matter and many younger people from many communities shutting down the SF Bay Bridge, showing up where the so called master and SFPD don't like and seeking justice for Mario Woods and his family. As a former leader of the San Francisco Black United Front, I congratulate and handover the power of the ancestors to the Nation of Islam as we as other civil and human rights activists seeking justice for the late Mario Woods and his family. May the struggle for justice continue however may police brutality, police terror and police murder end in the most modern and racist country in the world.

When we practice the type of unity as described in the book American Challenges in the Obama Era by Larry Ukali Johnson-Redd subtitled Moving toward a Strategic National Black Consensus, we will be able and empowered to launch a truly national or nationwide campaign to redefine policing to prioritize African American and others human rights over what we have now i.e. unchecked police bill of rights, rogue police excused for murder and brutality as well as voter suppression. With operational unity across all of our communities described by the Strategic National Black Consensus but needing the input of our activists and people where ever we come from or live in the USA we can fight harder nationally! Larry Ukali Johnson-Redd. Read the first 10 pages free@amazon.com/kindle

Subject: RE: Check out "Journey To The Motherland – From San Francisco to Benin City" - Novel by Larry Ukali Johnson-Redd

http://www.amazon.com/Journey-Motherland-Francisco-Benin- City/dp/0967422639

I warmly recommend this African Brother, Larry Ukali Johnson-Redd, and his insightful book, "*Journey To The Motherland – From San Francisco to Benin City*", to you all.

I read the book - and it is truly worth reading, the memorable journey of an African brother who ended up through the vagaries of human history (and the atrocities of the 'Middle Passage'), an American, but who nevertheless embarked on *a unique Journey of Self-Re-Discovery - the need to re- discover the AFRICAN in his African-American self*!

I read the book, twice over - and I still have and cherish my own *author- signed copy* of the book.

Dr. Valentine Ojo
Tall Timbers, MD

> Buy the copy from the author through Amazon.com ($4.00) and I will autograph your copy personally! I Immigrated to Nigeria from 1977 to 1981. Read this book to celebrate African-American History Month. This book is also an e-book available at Amazon.com/kindle for $ 2.99.

Sincerely,

Larry Ukali Johnson-Redd

None of the Wall Street crooks of 2008 went to jail while the Prison Industrial Complex and school to prison pipeline greatly increased through mass incarceration. For us as a people this is the Obama Era in 2015.

🕐 6 Years Ago Today

Larry Ukali Johnson-Redd

October 25, 2009·

I advise President Obama to collect the 1 Trillion Dollars back as soon as possible from those recipients who owe before 1 mega bonus is given out. I advise that the 1 trillion be spent to help fund Stimulus ll aimed at the states and Washington DC, like California and the other states with deficits, small business grants to hire Stimulus ll implementation workers and the creation of a National Adult Job Corps!

Trump's acceptance speech at the Republican Convention was full of white Supremacy and short on details claiming to be the law and order man but no mention of African American Police terror victims.

U.S. Rep. Frederica Wilson, who represents the area, said she was in shock.

"From what I saw, he was lying on the ground with his hands up. Freezing. But he was still shot," said Wilson, a Democrat

That was a quote from ABC news by a local congresswoman from North Miami several hours before the fiery Donald Trump GOP Convention speech. This could have offered the white supremacist Donald Trump an excellent opportunity to balance his white supremacy based GOP acceptance speech to balance his support of law enforcement with concern for African American human rights violations however Donald choose to ignore the daily news and the trending murder and shooting of African Americans and Latinos in ever rising numbers.

Charles Kinsey was shot with his hands raised while trying to get an Autistic man back to his secured location by police sent to the scene.

And when Charles survived and asked the police who shot him why was he shot? He got a dazed and confused answer like I don't know. The fact is that Charles Kinsey is one of the luckiest victims of police terror in years because although he was shot with his hands in the air, unarmed while lying on the ground and on a mission of mercy as a therapist recovering a patient, he survived!!!!!!! He is one of few African American victims left to tell the story from his on side of things. Usually there are so many bullets fired that survival is not possible.

Donald Trump gave his fiery one sided white supremacy speech without any sympathy expressed for the families of the late Freddy Gray or the family of the late Sandra Bland, or 12 year old Tamir Rice killed in Cleveland by police terror where the convention was held. Why such a silence on this growing number of Black victims of American police terror on Black Citizens? Coast to coast in the USA Black victims cry out for justice but despite Donald Trump saying he is the "voice" for people victimized by the system we are left to conclude the growing number of black and brown victims is not who Trump was referring to. Instead Trump is a white supremacist like Richard Nixon, and Ronald Reagan and his supporter David Duke formerly of the Ku Klux Klan. That is what can be observed when Donald Trump declares himself a Law and Order man whatever the police do.

That is why my message to African-Americans is to further develop my proposed Strategic National Black Consensus to define our relationship as a people to each other and our relationship to this white supremacy state called America to make the Strategic National Black Consensus into a South African style Freedom Charter or British style Magna Carta to define our need to be liberated in this hypocritical American democracy and codifying our need for full respect for our human rights as people and middle passage survivors. We need to produce that document emphasizing Human Rights and demanding an end to American police terror in the Obama Administration or any future American government as well setting down a basis for ending Black on Black disrespect and Black on Black crime. We also need to determine if a new US constitution is worth fighting or pushing for and what are we willing to do if police terror continues to shorten our numbers with no redress or appropriate justice and equal rights. We must fight for a nationwide Human Rights- Bill of Rights as part of National Legislation to eliminate police brutality. Also we should consider making all city and county police either state employees or federal employees so that new federal law enforcement with upgraded national standards beyond current standards developed with all stakeholder's impute because so many people of color and Black People are having any notion of human rights denied by current national police practices.

This national Human Rights legislation must be considered over police bill of rights in states like Maryland that give police for example 10 days of vacation after they kill someone in the line of duty without having to respond to any government officials about the killing while family and even law enforcement questions are second to police rights. This is not a police rights state but a people's rights state or at least it should be. And this state of police brutality must end for all people especially for African Americans and Latinos/Mexicans. Trump and other white Americans are again in denial and maybe if man white Americans were victimized by police brutality they would be more empathetic or able to feel what is a general feeling among police brutality victims. families and progressive supporters. The denialist stance of Trump leads him to say like Nixon before him is he is a law and order man, that is why progressives of all types must mobilize to give Trump a landslide defeat by voting against Trump. What we vote for may be Hillary Clinton but also for a progressive program because if you want a really progressive program as progressives we are going to have to fight for that program for the next 8 years at least.

So the end to deadly and brutal police brutality is progressive agenda issue/ item number 1 for progressives in the name of respect for human rights. Item number 2 is dramatic immigration reform including an amnesty for all current immigrants. We could or could not allow for the closure of all US borders however there must be an immediate halt to the deportations and family separations of immigrant families of nearly

11 million US taxpaying immigrants. These continuing deportations are also systematic human rights violations and that takes the US down the road of Nazi atrocities of the thirties and forties that happened to the Jews in Europe when they were deemed non white and therefore and/or less than pure white meaning less than human like many new majority people of today are marginalized. The rest of the progressive agenda must include Marshall Plan scale reconstruction including rebuilding national and community infrastructure of America's inner cities and rural development for rural areas because the economic oppression and profit taking of the elite 1% have left the national and community economy in shatters. And the lack of taxes on the rich does not leave any budget for the Marshall Plan scale rebuilding that is currently required. The 4th progressive agenda item but certainly not the least is a single payer system of healthcare. In simple words this means Medicare for all people in the USA from the cradle to the grave. It is no secret that all people need healthcare yet all too often poor or poorer people receive little to no healthcare in the most modern country in the world. Healthcare and Human Rights for all is really what makes a country modern.

So new majority people and all real progressives these proposals can form the basics of a progressive agenda. So long as we fight for proposals like these together as African Americans, Latinos/Mexicans, Asians, immigrants and other progressive members of the new majority, then we can vote for Hillary Clinton, but realize preventing the conservatives like Trump take over must be our first priority and our second priority would be struggling with Hillary Clinton, the corporate democrats and the status quo for the progressive agenda some many of us need for our survival. Then if we progressives and new majority can establish this positive rebuilding atmosphere in America so that we do better in the post Obama era as a people and as people of all types.

However the most important priority for African Americans whether this progressives stuff develops or not is the establishment of a Strategic National Black Consensus and National Black Trust to build up our survival options we need so badly in every Black community in

America so we can begin to produce peace among us as a people, end gang and internal wars against ourselves and empower our selves so we can be a basic foundation of the new majority in the immediate future. It is the poverty and history of maltreatment and to be more specifically the bad treatment of African Americans as well as the self hatred bred into African Americans by slavery, played up by white media and police have contributed as much as anything we bring to it are the foundations of the negative on- going war against ourselves that we participate in too much. So my people first let us unite with ourselves and agree to support the progressive agenda for progress. We need to empower ourselves so we can fight against corporate gangsters like Donald Trump and his buddies who are the 1 percent rich people, owners of private prisons, chain gang profiteers and the school to prison pipeline backers. We can defeat those who want to continue to oppress us but we first have to come together to empower ourselves. So we all have challenges in the Obama era as well as this time that will replace the Obama Era.

Before Hillary

Before Hillary there was a presentation of Mothers of the Movement. There was a short video clip shown with Hillary spending some quality time with these mothers of violence of the state the mothers of the movement included mothers of many of the young people we speak of as victims of police /prison guard terror like the mother of Sandra Bland, the mother of Jordon Davis, the mother of Mike Mike of Ferguson, Missouri and the mothers of Trayvon Martin and the mother of Eric Gardener and there were a few more. The mothers indicated Hillary had done some work understanding the murder of their sons and daughters,. Obviously that was something that Trump had no empathy for when he said he was a law and order man. Trump as far as Black lives mattering is completely one sided on the side 100 % on the side of good and bad cops. And when Trump says nothing to express sympathy with African American or Latino men and women suffer at the hands of bad police, Trump victimizes our victims again.

Mothers of the Movement made America look at the murder of our sons and daughters by bad police. These presentations of the mothers confront a white majority like Trump in complete denial as though there is a legitimate war against Black and Brown people. I put their presentation on my face book page to honor the mothers for banding together as a group and speaking out and seeking social justice. We all need to make sure a 12 year old Tamir Rice should not be killed by local POLICE WITH A TOY GUN IN A PARK. No African American indicated a discussion that said white lives did not matter however looking at the victims mothers one must understand that people are asking that their children not be being shot by bad police on or off videotape. Stop being in denial- white America after 500 years of slavery and oppression of African Americans and others. It was African American and Mexican lives were beginning to look like collateral damage as though our human rights did not matter. That is what spawned the sentence Black Lives Matter not the other way around.

We African American people like people are righteous people and realize all lives matter however after all the police terror in our communities cause us to say our lives matter. So it is white America that has to come out of denial and realistically prepare to help stop police terror anywhere in America. White America also has to realistically begin a discussion and studies on what type of reparations for African Americans would be appropriate in this day and age of the grandchildren of American slaves in unmarked graves.

I looked to both centrist presidents Bill Clinton and Barack Obama give serious long endorsement speeches praising Hillary Clinton. Both speeches were convincing and provided insight on the Hillary they knew but the presentation of the mothers of the movement did more than anything to show me a contrast from Trump. Despite the fact that President Obama is the subject of this book, I had to look at what came before Obama-Former President Bill Clinton and Barack Obama the current President. In looking at Hillary we look at what may be coming in the new future after the Obama Era. Clinton looked at a young radical Hillary and Barack Obama provided an inside look into the Senator Clinton and Secretary of State Hillary

No African American ever said Blue lives didn't matter however too many times the blue Gang had shot African Americans is questionable circumstances with a blue line of silence about the real story and the video screens lately showed exactly what happened in a growing number of police homicides. However progressives and new majority activists must be focused on the progressive goals and programs and not Clinton's centrist leanings to make real progressed like ending deadly police brutality and the revitalizing of our communities.

We African American are conscious people and that is why we know not only do Back Lives Matter but all lives matter however we have to be treated liked police respect our human rights. We too deserve that respect from the people in blue.

As Hillary begins her case I remember the old American adage about American candidates run from the left but govern from the center. That certainly was the case for both Presidents Clinton and Obama. However Hillary claims she respects Berni Sanders and his progressive proposals so we all will soon see. If Hillary runs to the left and then begins to rule without the input of progressives like the mothers of the movement this progressive movement and new majority will need to revolt against Hillary and pursue our progressive agenda until the progressive agenda is enacted into law. In summary Hillary first said and explained we have to work together to rise together. We will see and soon too.

Hillary speaks on: Immigration reform and a path to citizenship for immigrants already contributing to society. Hillary says stronger together more than once. However if the police terror and murder doesn't stop there will be bigger division .Hillary promises a better deal for all working people despite her connections to wall street but is not detailed as she could be. I see many progressive frowns as the camera pans the crowd among the enthusiastic supporters.

Hillary says when Barriers are cleared for everyone the shy is the limit. She promises policies to take money out of politics She further states Wall Street will not be allowed to ruin main street. She promises work to overturn Citizens United.

Hillary promises pro living wage advocacy and health care for all but if she said Medicare for all. She said " the economy has to work for all of us". She said in the first 100 days she promises to make investments in new jobs in new jobs new jobs and free education for the middle because 1% er's will pay higher taxes to create new jobs.

Hillary thumps Trump many times including Trump' selling his furniture made overseas as his way of putting America first is one. She thumps Trump on his ties to the gun lobby .She says we need to heal. Yes because we African Americans feel like we in a war the way we are addressed by some police and some racists. She says we need to heal the wounds that divide us and rebuild trust. We have not yet began the amount of dialog that could produce a deal because law enforcement like society has yet decided to respect our fundamental human rights signed by Franklin Roosevelt's wife, Eleanor Roosevelt. She says she will fight for human rights, women's rights and disability rights. Hillary even mentions prison reform but progressives and new majority it is very important to know what you want because there are no details much like Trump. Her appeal as she ends is we are stronger together. Hillary spoke 55 minutes while Donald spoke 75 minutes.

The new majority including African Americans and progressives should vote for Hillary for president and help make the reality of the first woman President in U.S. History. However Progressives and new majority including Asians should join together and organize a political interest group of some type including democratic progressives so that together we can bring about a ring of fire to keep Hillary's feet to the fire in favor of our progressive Agenda and programs as well as world peace because few details were provided in her nomination acceptance speech. The truth is the Trump speech also gave few details although you know Trump is a 1% political interest's candidate. However when Trump says he will be a law and order man with his buddies we Black,

Brown and young men and women already feel the wrath of law enforcement bad apples shooting, and killing our people under many times video and questionable circumstances to say the least Donald Trump with no empathy for us disqualifies himself from receiving our votes. This is the continuing story 500 years old of the search of my people from Africa and born in America for human rights and a part of that justice for all. Remember there are some of our young people saying give me freedom or give me death. That's been said before but the too great incarceration rate for our numbers and rich people making profits on private prisons is profit taking and racist white supremacy mix out of control that threatens to derail or destroy this democracy by the tyranny of the white, right and 1 percent wealthy people.

Freedom Delayed and the road to Dallas and Baton Rouge

What happens when
Freedom is delayed
And for hundreds of years
Your people are slaves

And the direct contradiction
Between Democracy and
White supremacy adds up to
Equals hypocrisy

And freedom, development and
respect delayed
for the majority
of descendents of the American Slave

Ex slaves in graves
Never had any rights
The road to Dallas and Baton Rouge.
Is a history of police brutality

The denial of our human rights
Is building an explosive Black rage
Our rights, bodies and minds
Are in a white supremacy cage

So we shout aloud
Black lives too matter
But the police terror/ murder
List gets fatter and fatter

Late Sandra Bland and the late Freddie Gray
Mike Mike Brown, Tamir Rice and Mario Woods
The list of victims is too long
And in a real democracy police terror, murder/brutality is wrong

First Baton Rouge then Minnesota
The rages builds and explodes in Dallas and Baton Rouge
500 hundred years of colonialism and slavery, kidnapping, rape,
murder and oppression racism white supremacy and police brutality

Where is the national legislation
And/or laws preventing racist police brutalization
Where is equal rights and justice
Not just for us whiter but for all of us

Police terror throughout American Land
Police brutality/murder/horror on
The Black and Brown man and women
Is the cause please understand